JOHN GAY:
THE BEGGAR'S OPERA

by PETER ELFED LEWIS

EDWARD ARNOLD

First published 1976 by
Edward Arnold (Publishers) Ltd
25 Hill Street, London W1X 8LL

ISBN cloth: 0 7131 5895 6
paper: 0 7131 5896 4

Printed in Great Britain by
The Camelot Press Ltd, Southampton

General Preface

The object of this series is to provide studies of individual novels, plays and groups of poems and essays which are known to be widely read by students. The emphasis is on clarification and evaluation; biographical and historical facts, while they may be discussed when they throw light on particular elements in a writer's work, are generally subordinated to critical discussion. What kind of work is this? What exactly goes on here? How good is this work, and why? These are the questions that each writer will try to answer.

It should be emphasized that these studies are written on the assumption that the reader has already read carefully the work discussed. The objective is not to enable students to deliver opinions about works they have not read, nor is it to provide ready-made ideas to be applied to works that have been read. In one sense all critical interpretation can be regarded as foisting opinions on readers, but to accept this is to deny the advantages of any sort of critical discussion directed at students or indeed at anybody else. The aim of these studies is to provide what Coleridge called in another context 'aids to reflection' about the works discussed. The interpretations are offered as suggestive rather than as definitive, in the hope of stimulating the reader into developing further his own insights. This is after all the function of all critical discourse among sensible people.

DAVID DAICHES

Contents

For Professor Jacques Blondel and my colleagues and students at the
University of Clermont, France, 1974–5

1 Introduction

At first sight, *The Beggar's Opera*, written in 1727 and produced in January 1728, may seem a fairly straightforward work, and its immediate attractiveness is undoubtedly one of its virtues; but the apparent simplicity is deceptive. The fact that stage productions vary so much in tone, from the near-tragic to the near-farcical, from the savagely satirical to the quasi-romantic, is sufficient evidence to establish that this is a play of many layers and facets, each of which can be emphasized at the expense of the others by a director. Like many works of art that have stood the test of time, *The Beggar's Opera* is very diverse and complex, and consequently appeals in different ways to different generations. Indeed, difficulties arise as soon as one attempts to categorize it. To begin with, it is a highly individual kind of opera, but at the same time it is an anti-opera in that it burlesques Italian opera. Nowadays, it should be noted, *The Beggar's Opera* may be performed by singers who have to speak or by conventional actors who have to sing. It is also a low-life romance, which means that it inverts the normal aristocratic conventions of romance and must consequently be regarded as an anti-romance too. We are frequently faced with the question of whether the hero is really a hero or an anti-hero and of whether the two heroines are really heroines or anti-heroines. They are, in fact, both. Sometimes we laugh at them, sometimes we sympathize with them, and sometimes we seem to be laughing and sympathizing simultaneously. As these remarks suggest, *The Beggar's Opera* is essentially a comedy, but once again it is hard to define the kind of comedy since the realistic and the romantic are so inextricably blended. To call it a comedy of low life might suggest a mainly realistic and satirical treatment in the tradition descending from Ben Jonson, but the element of romantic pathos in the play indicates that it also has affinities with the romantic comedy and even tragicomedy of Shakespeare and his Jacobean successors. Yet there is no denying the strong satirical strain in *The Beggar's Opera*. Packed as it is with caustic allusions to current political events, leading national figures, and even the Hanoverian court, it seemed outrageously outspoken in 1728 and caused considerable offence to Sir Robert Walpole's Whig government. Moreover, Gay's political and social satire, being general as well as topical, has not lost its bite. Although *The Beggar's Opera* contains such apparently diverse elements, Gay has welded them together so ingeniously that the joins are invisible. The play does not fragment into an episode of satire followed by an episode of low-life romance followed by an episode of operatic burlesque and so on. On the contrary, the elements move in tandem so that when a character sings a song he may be contributing to the burlesque of Italian opera and to the political satire or romance, as well as to Gay's revolutionary conception of ballad opera. A full appreciation of *The Beggar's Opera* demands that its various strands be separated out by critical analysis; in the play itself they are closely interwoven. (All quotations from the play are taken from my edition listed in the bibliography, although the eighteenth-century conventions of italicization retained in that edition are not reproduced here.)

2 The Beggar's Opera *as Opera and Anti-opera*

'It must be allow'd an Opera in all its forms'

Today *The Beggar's Opera* is usually regarded as one of the very few great English plays of the eighteenth century and as one of the major literary works of the Augustan period; yet the title asserts unequivocally that it is an opera. This apparent discrepancy poses the question—what kind of opera? To Gay's contemporaries, the title of his work would at first have seemed as incongruous (although for a slightly different reason) as those of the mock-heroic poems, *The Rape of the Lock* and *The Dunciad*, by his friend Pope. Writing for an élite educated in the classics, Pope knew that the words 'The Rape of' would bring to mind 'The Rape of Leda' or 'The Rape of Helen' or 'The Rape of Lucretia', myths and stories about events that had wide-ranging repercussions of epic proportions, such as the Trojan War. 'The Rape of' produces expectations that are dashed by the rest of Pope's title referring to a lock of hair. Similarly *The Dunciad* recalls Homer's *Iliad* and Virgil's *Aeneid*, but Pope's title indicates that his poem is an inverted epic, not of heroes but of dunces. By the time Gay wrote

The Beggar's Opera in 1727, 'opera' in England had become virtually synonymous with Italian opera, a theatrical form characterized by great dignity and seriousness and peopled with mythological figures or personages of high rank from the distant past. That an 'opera' could be a 'beggar's' consequently amounted to a contradiction in terms. Gay's very title more or less announces that he is turning Italian opera upside down, that his own opera is both a burlesque of the Italian form and a radically new kind of English opera, indeed the first comic opera, since before Gay most operas were devoid of levity and none sported such a flippant and unlikely title as *The Beggar's Opera*.

In order to appreciate the rationale behind Gay's opera, it is necessary to know something about the history of opera in England during the preceding three-quarters of a century. Towards the end of the Interregnum, it was possible to get round the Puritan ban on the staging of plays by presenting in private houses dramatic works which featured musical accompaniment throughout. These established a form, the English dramatic opera, that survived the reopening of the theatres in 1660 following the restoration of the monarchy. After 1660, however, there was no need for the music to be sustained throughout in order to evade prosecution, and the all-sung pattern of the Interregnum operas, in which every word had to be set to music, was abandoned. In form, though not of course in content, the dramatic opera of the Restoration period resembles the modern musical more closely than modern opera, which derives from Italian opera. The music is intermittent rather than continuous and some of the dialogue is spoken rather than sung, but the musical sections, although embedded within the framework of a spoken play, are usually much more important than the non-musical sections. As far as content goes, on the other hand, English dramatic opera resembles Italian opera in that the world it presents is elevated and heroic rather than realistic. Early in the eighteenth century the popularity of dramatic opera waned, and even though a few English operas continued to hold the stage after 1710, the genre was rapidly supplanted by Italian opera.

Not long after the 1705 production of *Arsinoe*, the first Italianate opera to be staged in England, a vogue for Italian opera was developing. What did more than anything else to accelerate this development was Handel's visit to London in 1710 and his subsequent decision to stay there. Handel, a prolific composer of genius but also something of an opportunist, arrived at exactly the right time. He was immediately commissioned to write an Italian opera and obliged with *Rinaldo* (1711), the first of many popular successes he supplied to English audiences. From 1710 the new

Queen's Theatre was the home of Italian opera in England and became known as the Opera House. Furthermore, leading Italian singers were paid enormous sums to perform in London and, as 'stars', were figures of widespread public interest. In the year in which *The Beggar's Opera* was written, for example, the personal feud between the two leading ladies of Italian opera in London, Faustina Bordoni and Francesca Cuzzoni, provided a considerable amount of off-stage entertainment, especially as on one occasion it erupted on stage into mutual punching, scratching and hair-pulling.

The snobbish vogue for Italian opera and the idolizing of its principal performers soon produced a hostile reaction from some English intellectuals, who laughed at the male castrati singers, at the temperamental behaviour of the prima donnas, at the convention of recitative, at the lavishness of operatic productions, and at the fact that operas were sung in a language which was incomprehensible to most of the audience. To some extent such mockery can be put down to patriotic bias, but neo-classical critics like Addison and Dennis genuinely believed that the vogue for Italian opera posed a threat to the orthodox dramatic forms of tragedy and comedy as well as to the vitality of English music. One of the charges levelled against Italian opera was that its appeal was very superficial, delighting the ear and the eye but failing to supply the intellectual stimulus and spiritual nourishment afforded by the English dramatic tradition since the Elizabethans.

Gay himself was musical and did not dislike Italian opera in the way that his more doctrinaire neo-classical contemporaries did. Indeed, he even provided Handel with an operatic libretto, *Acis and Galatea*, about ten years before he wrote *The Beggar's Opera*. But during the 1720s he became alarmed at the ever-increasing popularity of Italian opera and its effect on English drama and music. 'As for the reigning Amusement of the town, tis entirely Musick,' he complains in a letter to Swift (3 February 1723), adding that 'folks that could not distinguish one tune from another now daily dispute about the different Styles of Hendel, Bononcini, and Attillio'. Just as Jane Austen objected much less to the Gothic novel *per se* than to the excessive seriousness with which it was taken by impressionable members of the reading public, Gay condemns not Italian opera but the completely uncritical theatregoers who had turned it into a fashionable cult. Jane Austen nevertheless felt that a corrective was necessary, and in *Northanger Abbey* wrote a book that is both a burlesque of Gothic fiction and a realistic novel in its own right. In conceiving *The Beggar's Opera* Gay did something very similar. He set out to combine burlesque of Italian opera with the creation of a rival form, a comic and distinctly English form of opera that quickly became known as ballad opera. This dual purpose explains the considerable difference between *The Beggar's Opera* and the few previous burlesques of Italian opera, which are aimed at very specific targets and do not attempt to transcend burlesque. Gay deliberately avoids direct parody and close burlesque because this might well have prevented him from achieving a self-sufficient 'opera' capable of standing as an independent work of art.

Musically, there are two great differences between *The Beggar's Opera* and Italian opera. Firstly, much of Gay's work consists of orthodox dramatic dialogue without any musical accompaniment, whereas all the words in Italian opera are sung; in this respect *The Beggar's Opera* resembles the English dramatic opera of the Restoration more closely than Italian opera. Secondly, apart from the Overture, the music for *The Beggar's Opera* was taken from pre-existing sources, whereas an Italian opera was an entirely new musical creation. For the sixty-nine songs in the play, Gay himself selected the melodies, most of which were well known. Forty-one of the airs have broadside-ballad tunes (this explains the term 'ballad opera') but others have tunes by such distinguished contemporary composers as Purcell and Handel; Air xx is actually sung to the music of a march in one of Handel's greatest operatic successes, *Rinaldo*. What Gay did—and this was his most daringly original stroke— was to put new wine into old bottles, substituting his own words for the familiar ones, though retaining and modifying phrases here and there. This gamble might have failed disastrously, but Gay did it so well that in no time at all dramatic hacks were churning out inferior imitations. In the years immediately following 1728, ballad operas and ballad farces darkened the air; and although Italian opera continued to be popular, it now had to compete with a new vogue. Whatever Gay may have thought of the progeny his masterpiece spawned, he had certainly succeeded in restoring English opera. Today 'opera' seems the wrong word, but in the case of *The Beggar's Opera*, the large number of songs together with their vital dramatic importance distinguish it from plays of the seventeenth and early eighteenth centuries containing incidental music and songs. There is nothing incidental about Gay's memorable songs, and to many people they are the glory of the work.

As has been noted, Gay's burlesque of Italian opera is for the most part indirect and non-parodic, but his burlesque purpose explains many features of *The Beggar's Opera*. In order to maintain a superficial resemblance to Italian opera, Gay adopts several of its formal characteristics, such as a three-act structure instead of the five-act structure invariable in full-length tragedies and comedies. Again, following the example of Italian opera and departing from the customary practice of orthodox drama, he dispenses with both prologue and epilogue, the conventional and completely detachable speeches preceding and following a tragedy or comedy that were often contributed by someone other than the author. Operas did not open with a prologue but with an instrumental overture, and Gay specifies that an overture should be played for *The Beggar's Opera*. For the first production, J. C. Pepusch, a German composer of theatre music, provided a suitable overture featuring the melody Gay chose for Air XLVII. Although Gay's use of speech instead of recitative is a significant departure from operatic practice, his actual lay-out of the airs corresponds to that of arias in an Italian opera. The sudden switching from speech to song and back again without any attempt to justify the interpolation of an air on realistic grounds, as is often done in orthodox drama, recalls the alternation of recitatives and arias in opera. There is a further correspondence to Italian opera in that not all of Gay's airs are solos, some being duets, one being a trio, and a few involving a chorus.

Gay goes to some pains to draw attention to these and other operatic parallels in his Introduction, which precedes the Overture and which is an essential part of his design in a way that the conventional prologue was not. In this short scene, the supposed author of the opera, the Beggar, explains his work to one of the actors, the Player, and claims that although written to celebrate the marriage of two English ballad singers it is to all intents and purposes an orthodox opera. Instead of announcing explicitly in his own voice that he is about to burlesque Italian opera, Gay chooses the much subtler satiric method, perfected by Swift, of adopting a 'mask' or 'persona', that of the Beggar, and speaking indirectly through him. The Beggar's seriousness is really Gay's sleight of hand; his words are undermined from within so that we do not take them at their face value. Gay's irony can be fully appreciated only in the light of what is to follow, but his gibe at Italian opera is unmistakable when the Beggar says, 'I hope I may be forgiven, that I have not made my Opera throughout unnatural, like those in vogue; for I have no Recitative.' The Beggar appears to be apologizing for not making his opera 'throughout unnatural', but by implication these words carry their own qualification and disapproval. Gay is clearly invoking the Augustan aesthetic yardstick of nature as a measure for exposing the limitations of Italian opera. The further implication that 'Recitative' in particular is unnatural is a complaint often levelled against Italian opera at the time. According to Addison, English audiences were at first 'wonderfully surprized to hear Generals singing the Word of Command, and Ladies delivering Messages in Musick' (*The Spectator*, no. 29).

The rest of the Beggar's speech can also be interpreted at two levels. He is pleased with himself for using 'the Similes that are in all your celebrated Operas', and the ones he lists do appear in *The Beggar's Opera*: 'The Swallow' in Air XXXIV, 'the Moth' in Air IV, 'the Bee' and 'the Flower' in both Air VI and Air XV, and 'the Ship' in both Air X and Air XLVII. What Gay implies, however, is that such similes have been rendered inexpressive in Italian opera by having been worked to death; after all, they are 'in all your celebrated Operas', which is more or less true since simile arias were exceedingly popular. Gay himself tries to revitalize them, to rinse them clean, by employing them in an unconventional context. The Beggar also seems to be proud of his 'Prison Scene which the Ladies always reckon charmingly pathetick'. As his words suggest, a prison scene was almost a *sine qua non* in an Italian opera and usually occurred at a high point of the dramatic action so that as much emotional appeal as possible could be wrung from it. The irony here lies in the fact that not just one poignant scene but almost half of *The Beggar's Opera* takes place in a prison, and in addition that the prison is not some historically or geographically remote one with romantic associations, but Newgate prison in the heart of London, exactly as it was at the time with all its petty corruptions and abuses. As regards 'the Parts', the Beggar's self-congratulation at achieving 'a nice Impartiality to our two Ladies, that it is impossible for either of them to take Offence' carries a more immediately topical irony, referring as it does to the current quarrel between Francesca Cuzzoni and Faustina Bordoni over operatic roles. In some Italian operas there are two heroines who are rivals for the hero's affections, and to avoid causing friction, composers like Handel had to ensure that there was no obvious imbalance between the two parts. Nevertheless, even if they could not actually 'take Offence', Francesca Cuzzoni and Faustina Bordoni tended to treat an opera in which they appeared together as a singing contest, vying with each other vocally instead of working as part of a team. This satirical reference to the prima donnas also serves to draw attention to the operatic parallel: *The Beggar's Opera* itself has two heroines, Polly Peachum and Lucy Lockit, who are rivals for the affections of the hero, Macheath. Indeed, the rivalry between Polly and Lucy alludes to that of the prima donnas and to that of the operatic roles they performed.

The Beggar claims that except for using speech instead of recitative his work 'must be allow'd an Opera in all its forms'; but by means of irony and by explicit references to beggars, to ballad singers, who were not particularly reputable, and to the notorious London parish of St Giles-in-the-Fields, the resort of thieves, highwaymen and prostitutes, Gay indicates throughout the Introduction that the content of *The Beggar's Opera* is totally unlike that of Italian opera. While in many respects Gay does adhere to the 'forms' of Italian opera, the world he presents is the very unoperatic one of St Giles-in-the-Fields. He completely inverts Italian opera, with its classical, mythological or similarly elevated narratives and its exotic atmosphere, by setting *The Beggar's Opera* very firmly in the criminal underworld of contemporary London. Theatregoers in 1728 would have recognized immediately that two of the major characters, Peachum and Macheath, were based on the best-known underworld figures of the early eighteenth century, Jonathan Wild and Jack Sheppard, both of whom had been executed less than four years before the first production of the work. One of the locations is the city's principal criminal prison, and death by hanging or transportation to the colonies is the fate that seems to await most of the characters. For them, the year is divided not into seasons but into the various sessions of the city's criminal court, the Old Bailey. Instead of a typical operatic hero such as Handel's Rinaldo, Gay provides the leader of a gang of highwaymen, Macheath, who is called 'Captain' but has no legitimate claim to the rank. And instead of two typical operatic heroines like the high-born Rossane and Lisaura in *Alessandro*, the opera which Handel wrote for Faustina Bordoni's London début in 1726, Gay supplies Polly Peachum, the daughter of an organizer of crime and a receiver of stolen goods, and Lucy Lockit, the daughter of the very corrupt chief jailor of Newgate. The sustained tussle between Polly and Lucy over Macheath is a low-life equivalent of that between Rossane and Lisaura over Alessandro (Alexander the Great) and of almost identical love-battles in other Italian operas, as well as being a satirical allusion to the real-life tension between the two sopranos who played these operatic rivals. Of the other characters in *The Beggar's Opera* almost all the men are criminals of one sort or another and almost all the women are whores. Just as Jane Austen's characters in *Northanger Abbey* are anti-types of the stereotyped figures of the Gothic novel as well as self-sufficient novelistic characters, Gay's characters are anti-types of operatic stereotypes as well as self-sufficient dramatic characters. *The Begger's Opera* is undoubtedly true to its title in that it controverts every normal operatic expectation. The nobility of character, dignity of conduct, and refinement of both sentiment and language characteristic of Italian opera are largely replaced by the attitudes, behaviour and idiom of the underworld.

However, Gay cleverly exploits, for burlesque as well as for other purposes, the discrepancy between operatic expectations and what he provides, especially in his treatment of his 'operatic hero' Macheath; thus he ensures that the burlesque level is not lost sight of behind the layers of social and political satire. In some ways Macheath acts and sounds like an operatic hero. The first words he *speaks*, 'Suspect my Honour, my Courage, suspect any thing but my Love' (I.xiii), have a distinctly heroic note, and Polly's reply, with its unquestioning assumption that her highwayman-husband is on a par with Hercules or Alexander the Great, makes the burlesque parallel explicit: 'I have no Reason to doubt you, for I find in the Romance you lent me, none of the great Heroes were ever false in Love.' Polly's father, even at the moment of arresting Macheath in II.v, makes an identical connection between his son-in-law and the sort of men normally presented as operatic heroes: 'Your Case, Mr Macheath, is not particular. The greatest Heroes have been ruin'd by Women.' Lucy too acknowledges the 'heroic' status of Macheath, as in her first remark on visiting him in the condemned cell: 'There is nothing moves one so much as a great Man in Distress' (III.xv). In his dealings with his gang, Macheath clearly sees himself as the equivalent of a military leader like Alexander and actually behaves with the magnanimity expected of an operatic hero. He claims to be brave, loyal, fair-minded, and generous: 'Is there any man who suspects my Courage? . . . My Honour and Truth to the Gang? . . . In the Division of our Booty, have I ever shown the least Marks of Avarice or Injustice?' (II.ii). And in III.iv, when two members of his gang are short of money after failing to steal anything, he keeps his word by digging into his own pockets: 'I am sorry, Gentlemen, the Road was so barren of Money. When my Friends are in Difficulties, I am always glad that my Fortune can be serviceable to them.' Here as elsewhere he addresses members of the gang as 'Gentlemen', insisting that they are all honourable: 'I have a fixt Confidence, Gentlemen, in you all, as Men of Honour, and as such I value and respect you' (II.ii) and 'But we, Gentlemen, have still Honour enough to break through the Corruptions of the World' (III.iv). In all such passages, the mock-heroic incongruity between the criminals who act, speak, and are spoken about, on the one hand, and the conduct and the sentiments expressed, on the other, registers as ironic burlesque.

Gay's use of familiar melodies, especially simple ballad tunes, as opposed to the elaborate arias of Italian opera is the musical equivalent of his making an operatic hero out of Macheath rather than someone like Alexander. The fact that the criminal characters of *The Beggar's Opera* burst into song in the manner of operatic figures in itself creates burlesque humour; and while it is unlikely that Gay intended to parody any specific arias, he does occasionally enhance the burlesque by making the hackneyed similes mentioned in the Introduction by the Beggar express attitudes, especially towards love, which are not found in the relatively chaste world of Italian opera. The simile of 'the Moth', for example, appears in Air IV, 'If Love the Virgin's Heart invade', in which Mrs Peachum reflects that if her daughter, like any other girl, 'plays about the Flame' and loses her virginity, she may end up as a whore—'Her Honour's sing'd, and then for Life, / She's—what I dare not name.' Gay also links operatic simile, in this case 'the Flower', with the fate of deflowered virgins in Polly's song about her politic motives for retaining her virginity, Air VI, 'Virgins are like the fair Flower in its Lustre'; this is intended to reassure her father that she knows how to 'grant some Things, and refuse what is most material', although she has in fact secretly married Macheath. In each of these songs the operatic simile is burlesqued by being made to convey non-operatic subject matter, but it is simultaneously rinsed clean in order to express a truth about the realities of contemporary life. The girl who succumbed to her sexual desires pre-maritally was, like the moth in the flame, quite likely to destroy herself. If she was known to have lost her virginity, she might well be cast out of the society that had nurtured her, and left to her own resources which usually meant prostitution. In Polly's song, Gay clarifies the severity of a social code that demanded such a penalty for a momentary human failing, and also conveys the fragility of virginity and the sense of sadness at its loss, by means of the very image which he is burlesquing. It is Gay's inspired juxtaposition of a natural garden and Covent Garden, which was a red-light district as well as London's vegetable, fruit, and flower market, that makes this possible. The cut flower ('once pluck'd, 'tis no longer alluring') being sent by the gardener to the market at Covent Garden signifies the deflowered virgin being virtually forced by society to the other Covent Garden, the flesh-market of the brothels ('There fades, and shrinks, and grows past all enduring, / Rots, stinks, and dies, and is trod under feet').

In other airs the discrepancy between what the simile normally conveys in opera and what it conveys in *The Beggar's Opera* is much less marked or even nonexistent; but because of the incongruity between the conceited linguistic idiom of opera and the unoperatic singer as well as the popular tune, the burlesque effect is still recognizable. Lucy's outburst of distress in Air XLVII, 'I'm like a Skiff on the Ocean tost', when she believes that Polly is 'sporting on Seas of Delight' with Macheath and decides on a plan of revenge as the only way to appease her jealousy, employs 'the Ship' simile mentioned by the Beggar in the Introduction; this therefore takes the form of an operatic cliché, for such outbursts of distress and jealousy were fairly common in Italian opera. Other airs, especially Polly's most tender expressions of devoted love for Macheath, also have operatic antecedents. Air XXXIV, 'Thus when the Swallow, seeking Prey', is the most obvious case since the Beggar points it out in speaking of the simile of 'The Swallow'; but Air XIII, 'The Turtle thus with plaintive crying', which is sung when Polly discovers that her parents are determined to arrange Macheath's execution and which features the conventional comparison of lovers to turtle-doves, is very similar. Shortly afterwards, Macheath and Polly are alone together for the first time in the play, and this scene (I.xiii), in which they declare their love for each other before having to part, contains no less than five airs, including three duets. The marked preponderance of song in itself indicates a parallel to operatic love scenes, and in his fine essay on the play, Bertrand H. Bronson tentatively suggests that Gay may have had in mind a scene between parting lovers in Handel's *Floridante* (1721); one of the duets (Air XVI) in particular bears some resemblance to the impassioned avowals of everlasting love by Elmira and Floridante (see bibliography).

Bronson argues that several other situations in *The Beggar's Opera* may have specific operatic sources. The way in which Macheath is arrested in a tavern (II.v) could be based on the attempt on Ptolemy's life in a seraglio in Handel's *Giulio Cesare* (1724), and the quarrel between Peachum and Lockit (II.x) possibly owes something to another scene between arguing fathers in Handel's *Flavio* (1723). In the latter case, however, the main source is the quarrel between Brutus and Cassius in Shakespeare's *Julius Caesar* and the similarity to the operatic scene may be no more than a coincidence. Whether Gay intended these very specific situational correspondences remains hypothetical. However, especially in the closing stages of *The Beggar's Opera* there are several unmistakable though general parallels with Italian opera, and these culminate in the *coup de théâtre* when the two characters from the Introduction, the Beggar and the Player, enter to produce a happy ending out of apparent catastrophe.

First of all there is Lucy's attempt to eliminate her rival, Polly, by poisoning her (III.vii–x). Having helped Macheath to escape from Newgate, Lucy is tormented by 'Jealousy, Rage, Love and Fear' because she believes, wrongly, that he is with Polly. Lucy has 'the Rats-bane ready', and when Polly comes to visit her at Newgate, Lucy suggests that they have a drink to cheer themselves up. But at the moment when Lucy forces a glass containing the poison on Polly, the recaptured Macheath is brought back to the prison and Polly is so shaken at the sight of him in chains that she drops the glass and spills its contents. Gay undoubtedly bases this episode on a popular feature of a number of contemporary Italian operas, the scene set in a prison in which one of the principal characters narrowly escapes death in the form of a cup of poison. These incidents take various forms, but in several of Handel's operas produced not long before The Beggar's Opera, the hero seems doomed to die by drinking a cup of poison yet is saved as a result of a last-second intervention during which the cup is upset. In Radamisto (1720), for example, the heroine Zenobia is forced by Tiridate to take a bowl of poison to her condemned lover, Radamisto himself, who is shackled and awaiting execution; but when she reaches him, she offers to drink it herself and is prevented only by the sudden entrance of Tiridate who knocks the bowl out of her hands. An almost identical scene occurs in Floridante. In Radamisto and Floridante, the gesture is one of heroic self-sacrifice, and the treatment is intensely emotional. In The Beggar's Opera, the action is a cunning and unheroic attempt to commit murder under the pretence of friendship, and the treatment verges on the comic. This whole episode has a further burlesque significance in that it resembles the encounters between rival operatic heroines, such as Rossane and Lisaura in Alessandro, where they attempt to discuss their relationships with the hero.

The burlesque parallel continues in the scenes following Macheath's return to Newgate. The kind of prison scene in Italian opera that 'the Ladies always reckon charmingly pathetick', to use the Beggar's phrase, is the one outlined above in which a woman visits her lover or husband who is awaiting death; the greater his suffering and her grief, the more 'charmingly pathetick' the scene would be. Earlier in The Beggar's Opera (II.xiii), Gay provides a counterpart to such scenes by exposing the imprisoned Macheath simultaneously to Polly and Lucy, each of whom regards herself as his wife. The result, a comic confrontation between a rake and two of his women, one of whom, Lucy, is pregnant by him, is the antithesis of the decorous intensity of operatic prison scenes; it also travesties the situation of a hero like Alessandro, who is faced with an almost impossible choice between Rossane and Lisaura. Macheath, under verbal bombardment from both Polly and Lucy, responds in the rollicking and impudent Air xxxv, 'How happy could I be with either', by deciding to ignore both of them. The operatic parallel is considerably reinforced by Gay's subsequent use of two duets in this scene. In Air xxxvi, 'I'm bubbled' ('bubbled' means 'deceived'), the vocal line passes back and forth between Polly and Lucy just as it does between the singers of operatic duets, especially rival heroines; but the situation from which the song arises, their discovery of Macheath's duplicity in making identical promises to both of them, is unlike anything to be found in Italian opera. Air xxxviii, 'Why how now, Madam Flirt?', in which Polly and Lucy attack each other verbally, differs in that the vocal line does not alternate throughout; instead Lucy sings the first stanza and Polly the second. Of particular interest here is the fact that the monosyllabic words at the end of the third line of each stanza, 'Dirt' and 'made', must be sung in melismatic or coloratura style, each word running for seventeen notes and occupying almost three bars. Such ornate, bravura singing is standard in operatic arias but very rare in folk songs and ballads, and is the only sustained example in *The Beggar's Opera*, where Gay usually fits one syllable to one note of music. That Gay should draw such attention to the operatic parallel in this song is doubly significant since nowhere else is the rivalry between Polly and Lucy so bitterly and vulgarly expressed. The contrast between matter and operatic manner is therefore exceptionally pronounced, and this in turn highlights the undignified personal behaviour of Francesca Cuzzoni and Faustina Bordoni in comparison with the dignified roles they took in operas. Off stage the prima donnas behaved as Polly and Lucy do on stage.

In the closing scenes Gay again brings Polly, Lucy, and Macheath together in Newgate after Lucy's attempt to poison Polly (III.xi). This encounter between the highwayman and his two 'wives' is less obviously a travesty of 'charmingly pathetick' prison scenes, but the continuing competition between the women for Macheath's attention, especially when it takes the form of a duet in Air LII, 'Hither, dear Husband, turn your Eyes', sustains the operatic burlesque. The way in which one voice takes over from the other like an echo in the second half of the song (''Tis Polly sues. / 'Tis Lucy speaks') imitates a feature of many operatic duets. As before, Macheath's predicament as expressed in Air LIII, 'Which way shall I turn me?—How can I decide?', is the essentially comic one of a philanderer, who is expert at handling one woman at a time, becoming helpless and retreating into silence when face to face with two of his conquests; again it alludes to the dilemma confronting Alessandro and some other heroes. If John O. Rees is correct in interpreting this scene as a mock-heroic version of the classical myth called The Judgment (or Choice) of Hercules, the burlesque resemblance to opera is greatly enhanced since Hercules was a very suitable candidate for operatic treatment (see bibliography). In the myth, Hercules is confronted by two goddesses, Virtue and Pleasure (or Vice), and has to decide between them. This subject was popular with creative artists from the Renaissance onwards because it allowed them to present a metaphysical and moral conflict as a dramatic and concretely-realized situation; in the eighteenth century it was treated by several poets and composers in England, including Handel. The symmetrical arrangement of Gay's characters, with Polly and her father on one side of Macheath, and Lucy and her father on the other, is very similar to the usual formal organization of painted versions of the myth and could well be modelled on them; but it would be wrong to push the parallel too far by identifying Polly with Virtue and Lucy with Pleasure.

As an interlude before the scene changes to the condemned cell, Gay specifies 'A Dance of Prisoners in Chains' at the end of III.xii. This plainly grotesque dance is a low-life counterpart to the dignified ballet dancing that had been incorporated in many operas since the seventeenth century, and the completely arbitrary way in which it is introduced is itself a comment on the frequent insertion of dances into operas with little or no dramatic justification. The burlesque intention is much more obvious here than in the 'Dance a la ronde in the French Manner' in II.iv, but although this may sound more formal and operatic, it is not performed by deities in a temple or by aristocrats in a court but by Macheath and eight whores in a tavern near Newgate. It too is introduced in a gratuitous way when Macheath hears harp music: 'But hark! I hear musick. . . . E'er you seat your selves, Ladies, what think you of a Dance?'

When the scene does change to the condemned cell (III.xiii), Macheath sings a soliloquy to music taken from no less than ten different songs so that the ten airs, LVIII–LXVII, coalesce into an extended piece of singing. Nowhere else in the play does Gay use fragments of tunes and nowhere else does one air follow another without any speech intervening. Of the ten airs, one consists of one line, six consist of two lines, two consist of four lines, and only the final one of eight lines is of average length. Despite the Beggar's initial claim that his opera contains 'no Recitative', Macheath's segmented utterance and abrupt changes of tune, interrupted .

only when he pours himself stiff drinks, is not unlike operatic recitative, especially as it concludes with a full-length air in the same way as recitative prepares the way for an aria. In opera such rapid changes of thought and emotion as Macheath's can be encompassed only in recitative, never in arias. From Gay's scrupulous avoidance before this of anything resembling recitative, one would expect the bulk of Macheath's monologue to be spoken; so the startling use of song is extremely effective in bringing home the operatic parallel. At the level of burlesque, Macheath's 'recitative and aria' is a mockery of those sung by operatic heroes in prison. Instead of exhibiting courage and fortitude while awaiting execution, like Floridante in Handel's opera who even welcomes death as a deliverance, the much more human Macheath drinks heavily in a not very successful attempt to go to the gallows bravely and concentrates his thoughts on alcohol and women.

The one sung trio, Air LXVIII, 'Would I might be hang'd!', occurs at what might be called the most 'charmingly pathetick' moment when Polly and Lucy visit Macheath in the condemned cell just before he is about to be taken to Tyburn to be hanged (III.xv). Since these three characters are on stage together in a number of scenes, there are several opportunities for trios; Polly and Lucy actually sing duets in front of Macheath, but only here do all three share an air. Gay is again following operatic precedent, because it is common in opera for the principal characters (if there are three) to join in a trio at the climax of the work. The cowardly but credible behaviour of Macheath, who has run out of alcohol ('I tremble! I droop!—See, my Courage is out'), is the antithesis of, for example, Floridante's operatic heroics in the face of death, and the yearning of both Polly and Lucy to share Macheath's fate on the gallows ('Would I might be hang'd! / And I would so too!') is a comic transformation of the attempts by self-sacrificing operatic heroines to kill themselves in order to save their lovers' lives. Gay's choice of tune for this 'Hanging Trio' could hardly have been better since 'All you that must take a Leap' was a ballad about the execution of two criminals. The burlesque effect is greatly intensified at this point by the sudden arrival of four more of Macheath's 'wives', each accompanied by a child, so that he is confronted by no less than six of his 'wives' and four of his children. Gay deliberately plunges what in opera would be intended to be a profoundly moving climax to the level of farce. Ironically, only in this ludicrous situation does Macheath acquire the moral strength of an operatic hero and welcome death as a deliverance: 'What—four Wives more!—This is too much.—Here—tell the Sheriffs Officers I am ready.'

The travesty of opera could hardly be taken further, yet Gay does just that in the next scene.

As Macheath is led away, the action is interrupted and the dramatic illusion shattered by the entry of the Player and the Beggar (III.xvi). This is a low-life equivalent of the device known as the *deus ex machina*, common in heroic drama, tragicomedy and opera after the Restoration, and involving a surprise intervention or unexpected discovery that produces a virtually magical transformation at a stroke. No matter how closely Italian operas approached tragedy, happy endings were *de rigeur*, and the contrived dénouements necessitated by this convention were particularly vulnerable to hostile criticism. At the end of *Arsinoe*, for example, Dorisbe stabs herself melodramatically after being rejected in love, but in no time at all she participates in the finale, explaining that her wound is not serious. In opera after opera the villain redeems himself at the end of the third act, and however diabolically he has behaved throughout, he suddenly becomes penitent and is reconciled with the other characters. In *The Beggar's Opera* the Player prevents the law taking its natural course by expostulating to the Beggar about Macheath's imminent execution. To the Player's surprise, the Beggar admits that he is 'for doing strict poetical Justice' with Macheath executed and all the other characters hanged or transported. But he gives way in the face of the Player's irrefutable argument:

Player Why then, Friend, this is a down-right deep Tragedy. The Catastrophe is manifestly wrong, for an Opera must end happily.

Beggar Your Objection, Sir, is very just; and is easily remov'd. For you must allow, that in this kind of Drama, 'tis no matter how absurdly things are brought about.—So—you Rabble there—run and cry a Reprieve—let the Prisoner be brought back to his Wives in Triumph.

Player All this we must do, to comply with the Taste of the Town.

The play can then end with a song and a dance to celebrate Macheath's release. What is so ingenious about this episode is that it allows Gay to criticize explicitly Italian opera and its fans, to burlesque by means of Macheath's reprieve the miraculous reversals of fortune and character with which operas frequently end, and at the same time to secure a fitting conclusion to what is, after all, a comedy. *The Beggar's Opera* demands a non-tragic ending, and in rescuing Macheath, Gay makes a virtue of necessity—indeed, several virtues. There is even a political innuendo in

Macheath's unexpected escape from death; during the difficult situation following George I's death in 1727, Sir Robert Walpole surprisingly avoided political extinction by promising the new king, George II, more money for the royal family. The burlesque is given an added pungency by the completely arbitrary nature of Macheath's reprieve, which is in no way earned and is not accompanied by any moral transformation. His promise of fidelity to Polly, 'I take Polly for mine . . . And for Life, you Slut,—for we were really marry'd' (III.xvii), cannot be taken too seriously considering the value of his earlier promises, not to mention his condescending though admittedly affectionate use of 'Slut'.

Today, Gay's burlesque of Italian opera seems much less significant than his social satire, which is more immediately accessible to us, and criticism of the play understandably concentrates on such literary qualities as irony and imagery. Nevertheless, Gay aimed to create an original type of opera by turning the conventions of Italian opera upside down so that he was simultaneously poking fun at them, and this attempt lies behind the overall structure of The Beggar's Opera and the detailed organization of many of its parts. The continuing popularity of the work means that it is possible to enjoy it without being aware that it burlesques Italian opera, just as it is possible to enjoy Northanger Abbey without knowing anything about the Gothic novel; but the subtlety and skill of Gay's design cannot be fully appreciated without grasping the extent to which he uses, mutatis mutandis, stock operatic features and situations. The Beggar's Opera is much more than a mock-opera, but at one level that is what it is. In addition, it is ultimately impossible to separate the social satire from the operatic burlesque since they are two sides of the same coin, as I hope to show later. To the literary critic, Gay's use of language is so absorbing that it is easy to forget that he wrote the play for the theatre and for part-musical performance. But the main reason that The Beggar's Opera appealed so much to theatregoers in 1728 and has held the stage ever since is not that it is a literary masterpiece, but that it is a lively and unconventional musical comedy, a kind of opera.

3 The Beggar's Opera *as Romance and Anti-romance*

'For I find in the Romance you lent me, none of the great Heroes were ever false in Love'

Swift's suggestion, in a letter to Pope (30 August 1716), that Gay should attempt 'a Newgate pastoral, among the whores and thieves there' is usually regarded as the seed from which *The Beggar's Opera* grew. This explanation is questionable, but its persistence indicates that even if it is not literally true it contains a significant truth, namely that the phrase 'Newgate pastoral' is a very apt description. (William Empson's important essay on the play is included in his book, *Some Versions of Pastoral*.) If Swift had written 'Newgate romance' he would have been even more accurate, but he used 'pastoral' because he almost certainly had a poem in mind. At the time, a 'Newgate pastoral' was as paradoxical as a 'beggar's opera', since the genre of pastoral was normally expected to deal with the idealized life and love of shepherds and shepherdesses in the golden age of antiquity, not with the actualities of contemporary country life, let alone urban life. The conventions of romance are similar in that the world presented is not realistic and contemporary but idealized and distanced, the heroes and heroines being intended to embody positive values such as nobility and virtue. Romance is peopled by aristocrats, not by criminals, and its characteristics include chivalry, delicacy of feeling, and a high style, not licentiousness, crudity, and the argot of the underworld. A 'Newgate pastoral' or 'Newgate romance' consequently suggests a forcing together of opposites, a reconciliation of what at first sight are irreconcilable.

Just as *The Beggar's Opera* is both a new kind of opera and an anti-opera, it is also a new kind of romance and an anti-romance. And since Italian opera usually conformed to the conventions of pastoral or romance and might be regarded as a musical species of these genres, the operatic and romance elements in *The Beggar's Opera* often overlap. Indeed, what has been said about Gay's inversion of the conventional operatic world applies equally well to his treatment of romance (although my treatment of opera does not exhaust the subject of romance). There is, for example, Macheath's attempt to wriggle out of a very awkward predicament when he is brought face to face with both Polly and Lucy in Newgate, and the even more unromantic situation when he is joined by six 'wives' and four bastards in the condemned cell. Gay's presentation of Macheath as an heroic 'Man of Honour' and of Polly and Lucy as heroines worthy of this 'great Man' is an outrageous mockery of romance conventions, but because these characters have positive identities as well as negative ones, *The Beggar's Opera* is more than an anti-romance. With his warm-heartedness, commitment to his gang, and anarchic zest for love and life, Macheath actually acquires the status of a hero—an unconventional, comic one; and with their undeviating devotion to him in spite of his unfaithfulness and broken pledges, both Polly and Lucy become genuine heroines—equally unconventional, of course. By transferring the romance world to Newgate, Gay achieves not only burlesque, but a highly unorthodox low-life romance in which the apparent dregs of society are treated as very human people in their own right who are just as worthy of literary attention as the noblemen of romance. Gay urbanizes romance and, in so doing, makes it truly democratic—of the people, not of the aristocracy.

Gay's blend of romance and low life is succinctly illustrated in Air III, 'If any Wench Venus's Girdle wear', which Mrs Peachum sings after explaining to her husband that women 'are so partial to the Brave that they think every Man handsome who is going to the Camp or the Gallows' ('the Camp' refers to military service). The common criminal about to be hanged from the 'cart', which was used to transport condemned prisoners from Newgate to the gallows at Tyburn, 'hath the Air of a Lord', for Mrs Peachum; moreover, he is glamorously transformed into a romance figure, a contemporary equivalent of Adonis, the beautiful youth in Greek mythology who was loved by Venus ('And we cry, There dies an Adonis!'). Gay is not, of course, advocating Mrs Peachum's view wholeheartedly, but neither is he completely discrediting her. Such transformations sometimes happened in real life, notably in the case of Jack Sheppard on whom Macheath is partly modelled. Sheppard's escapes from the condemned cell in Newgate made him legendary, and when he was finally taken to Tyburn through the streets of London, he was greeted with the sort of reception usually reserved for conquering heroes on their return home. What Gay is suggesting is that the low-life or criminal character is not simply the antithesis of the romance character. The mock-heroic parenthesis, '(A Rope so charming a Zone is!)', with its deliberate incongruity between what is described and the language used to describe it, itself epitomizes the way in which two apparently alien and mutually exclusive worlds are brought together. The hangman's rope is not only said to be 'charming' but also called 'a Zone', a refined poeticism for 'girdle' or 'encircling band' that refers to 'Venus's Girdle' in the first line of the song; anyone putting on Venus's magic girdle, even an ugly, low-life 'Wench', immediately became very attractive.

The theme of love, which is just as important here as in romance, pastoral, and Italian opera, is sometimes presented by Gay in an almost vehemently anti-romantic way, although the stylization resulting from the use of music and mock-heroic humour does mute the effect. From the opening, references to relationships between the sexes are often marked by extreme cynicism, the attitude of Peachum and Lockit towards almost everything. It is Peachum who utters the first of the many animal images used to define human beings and their activities. 'I love to let Women scape', he says when he decides to arrange Betty Sly's acquittal on criminal charges, but there is nothing altruistic in his behaviour since, like the hunter or gamekeeper in the metaphor he employs, he disparagingly regards the female of the species as mere breeding-stock: 'A good Sportsman always lets the Hen Partridges fly, because the breed of the Game depends upon them' (I.ii). For Peachum, women like Betty Sly serve a useful purpose in providing a good supply of criminals for the future. Then, commenting on the fact that the reward of forty pounds for information leading to a criminal conviction and probable execution applied only to male felons, Peachum observes wittily but sardonically that 'there is nothing to be got by the Death of Women—except our Wives'. Implicit in his subsequent aphorism that 'Surgeons are more beholden to Women than all the Professions besides' is the view that sex is a marketable product bringing financial benefit not only to the immediate vendors, prostitutes, but also to more respectable members of society, doctors, who could make a lot of money out of treating venereal disease and were consequently grateful to prostitutes for transmitting it. Gay himself is undermining that respectability with his suggestion that 'the Surgeons' are just as parasitic as brothel-keepers and pimps. In III.vi, the tallywoman Mrs Trapes, who supplies clothes to whores on credit, complains that she has as many as 'eleven fine Customers now down under the Surgeon's Hands'.

The suggestions implicit in Peachum's remarks are made fully explicit in

Air II, ''Tis Woman that seduces all Mankind', sung by Filch, who is serving an 'apprenticeship' to Peachum as a pick-pocket and thief and who is therefore very appropriately named. This song is so important because it establishes at the outset of the play a conception of love that is taken for granted by several of the characters but that is the converse of the courtly ideals of love found in romance. That love might be an ennobling or refining experience, that it might have anything to do with tenderness, joy, or mutual devotion and esteem, that it might be more than an ejaculation into a sensually attractive hunk of flesh, is evidently not worthy of consideration. Love, for Filch, is a machiavellian game in which one individual is pitted against another until a bargain is struck so that the man obtains momentary sexual gratification and the woman some kind of material reward. Sexual or any other kind of harmony between man and woman would not seem to be a possibility even as a by-product. Behind Filch's song is the Old Testament myth of the Fall, but Eve and the Serpent are rolled into one so that Adam has absolutely no chance. Women devote themselves to the deception of men ('seduces . . . wheedling Arts . . . cheat . . . tricks'), and since men cannot resist these feminine temptations or are unable to control their sexual impulses, they become easy victims. As men succumb, they are reduced to the level of beasts ('like Wolves') and are contaminated by female wiles so that they too 'practise ev'ry Fraud'. Because love is a commercial transaction ('Beauty must be fee'd into our Arms') rather than an interpersonal relationship, men are forced into crime ('by night we roam for Prey') in order to obtain sufficient money to pay for what they are duped into wanting. Adam is well and truly expelled from the Garden of Eden into the waste land of the city, but the blame rests almost entirely on Eve-Serpent. Yet when sung to a popular tune in performance, Filch's words do not come over in as unequivocally anti-romantic a way as they would if spoken. The music softens the bleak, cynical content even though it makes the departure from operatic arias about love very obvious.

In the course of the play several characters echo Filch's views, either in word or deed. The idea of men being the victims of women, for example, recurs frequently. Macheath is betrayed by two of his prostitute friends, Jenny Diver and Suky Tawdry, while they are flirting with him in a tavern, and after arresting him Peachum describes women as 'a pretty sort of Creatures, if we could trust them' (II.v), thus confirming Macheath's outburst about their essential deceitfulness, 'Women are Decoy Ducks'. Macheath's more considered reflection on this betrayal in Air XXVI, 'Man may escape from Rope and Gun', also employs animal imagery, woman being identified with the deadly mythological creature known as the basilisk or cockatrice ('That Basilisk is sure to kill'), which was hatched by a serpent from a cock's egg and whose gaze was fatal. Man ('The Fly') is again seen as completely at the mercy of the unmerciful but irresistibly attractive being, woman ('The Fly that sips Treacle is lost in the Sweets'). The repetitions of 'Woman' in 'he that tastes Woman, Woman, Woman, / He that tastes Woman, Ruin meets' hammer home the point that no man is immune from female treachery; they also reinforce Peachum's words at the time of the arrest about Macheath's fate being typical rather than unique since even 'The greatest Heroes', with whom Peachum seems to equate Macheath, 'have been ruin'd by Women' (II.v). Although Macheath escapes from Newgate with the help of a woman, Lucy, her father is convinced that Macheath's fondness for the sex will lead to his early recapture. In III.v, Lockit tells Peachum that by keeping 'a watchful Eye upon Polly' they will soon lay hands on Macheath again because women invariably cause the downfall of men, as he explains in Air XLV, 'What Gudgeons are we Men!'; figuratively, 'Gudgeons' (small fresh-water fish that are very easy to catch) are people who will swallow anything, even 'the Hook', and so are 'Ev'ry Woman's easy Prey'.

Another anti-romantic aspect of man-woman relations stressed in Filch's song, the connection between love and money ('For Suits of Love, like Law, are won by Pay'), is sustained throughout. 'Money well tim'd, and properly apply'd, will do any thing', claims Macheath in II.xii, and although he is thinking specifically of bribing his way out of Newgate, he applies his proposition to amorous intrigues in the ensuing song, Air XXXIII, stating that it is 'The Perquisite softens her into Consent'. Between Macheath's escape and recapture, Lockit encounters Filch himself in Newgate and is alarmed at his physical appearance: 'Why, Boy, thou lookest as if thou wert half starv'd; like a shotten Herring' (III.iii). When Filch explains why he looks so worn out, the appropriateness of Lockit's comic simile of a herring that has spawned, yet another animal image, becomes clear. Female prisoners awaiting trial frequently took the precaution of becoming pregnant so that if convicted of a capital offence they could 'plead their bellies' and so escape the death penalty. Filch has been earning 'a little Money by helping the Ladies to a Pregnancy against their being call'd down to Sentence'. He has quite literally been making a business out of sex, obviously to the detriment of his health and without much enjoyment: 'But if a Man cannot get an honest Livelyhood any easier way, I am sure, 'tis what I can't undertake for another Session.'

Gay's burlesque of romance is made explicit in this scene when Lockit describes 'the favourite Child-getter' of Newgate as a chivalric hero: 'The Vigor and Prowess of a Knight-Errant never sav'd half the Ladies in Distress that he hath done.'

Since most of the women in the cast are whores, sex is also their business, and very businesslike and mercenary they are. None of them conforms to the sentimental cliché of the streetwalker with a heart of gold; rather, their hearts are devoted to gold in the form of hard cash. Mrs Coaxer praises Jenny Diver's ability to pick the pockets of her customers 'as cooly, as if Money were her only Pleasure' (II.iv). Suky Tawdry tells how the last man who kept her abandoned her when he discovered that she had stolen five guineas from him, and later explains that she prefers old men 'for we always make them pay for what they can't do'. And Mrs Vixen sings the praises of apprentices because 'they bleed freely', meaning they spend lavishly and are soon parted from their money. Macheath himself, who according to Mrs Trapes 'is very generous to the Ladies' (III.vi), is a regular frequenter of their company and a good client. When arrested he is carousing with no fewer than eight of them in a tavern, and he is subsequently recaptured while with Mrs Coaxer after being accosted by her on his way to meet his gang. It is shortly after parting very tenderly from Polly that he surrounds himself with the prostitutes in an attempt to overcome his gloom at being pursued by Peachum—the latter in his role of thief-taker working for the law. 'I must have Women', Macheath declares, 'There is nothing unbends the Mind like them' (II.iii), and while awaiting their arrival, he confesses to his highly promiscuous nature:

> I love the Sex. And a Man who loves Money, might as well be contented with one Guinea, as I with one Woman. The Town perhaps hath been as much oblig'd to me, for recruiting it with free-hearted Ladies, as to any Recruiting Officer in the Army.

Gay's ambivalence towards romance is very much in evidence in these words and in the subsequent tavern scene (II.iv). On the face of it, Macheath's attempt to drown his sorrows in wine and women could be nothing if not sordid and the height of anti-romantic, especially since he has just been promising Polly that he would never be false to her and, furthermore, since the scene ends with his betrayal to the forces of law and order by two of the whores, who feign great affection for him in order to take him off his guard. This scene could have been one of sinister gloom and joyless depravity, incorporating a sermon about the destructive power of lust and some cant about fallen women being unhappy and degraded victims of society. Whether the prostitutes in the play are actually happy is arguable, but they are certainly content with their lot and are not lacking in gaiety and exuberance. They may be money-grubbing, but they also possess an infectious energy that rapidly restores Macheath's spirits, as he predicts in Air XXI, 'If the Heart of a Man is deprest with Cares, / The Mist is dispell'd when a Woman appears.' In spite of the plot against Macheath by Jenny Diver and Suky Tawdry, there is an element of amoral exhilaration and sheer animal vitality in this tavern scene. Even Air XXIII, 'Before the Barn-door crowing', Jenny Diver's song about the barnyard morals of the characters appropriately couched in barnyard imagery, has a positive as well as a negative dimension. The use of the sustained metaphor of the crowing cock and his hens to expound man-woman relationships, those of Macheath and his prostitute friends ('The Cock by Hens attended'), is plainly anti-romantic and takes its place in a sequence of such images. (It must be emphasized, however, that not all the animal images carry this kind of connotation, Polly's use of turtle doves in Air XIII and swallows in Air XXXIV, for example, having an exactly contrary significance.) Yet Jenny Diver's song is not simply a moral accusation. Indeed, it is, in a way, almost celebratory. The repetition of 'how do you do' in the last two lines ('With how do you do, and how do you do, / And how do you do again'), with its suggestion of repeated intercourse and multiple orgasm, reinforces the words of the previous line, 'And cheers the happy Hen'. After making his choice from the Hens at his disposal, Macheath's sexual performance as Cock actually 'cheers' the Hen, whoever she is, and makes her 'happy'. Human love may reach higher and richer forms than Macheath and his bevy of whores are capable of, but they evidently achieve something more rewarding than, to take a modern example, the manifest non-fulfilment of the living dead in all those arid sexual encounters in T. S. Eliot's early poems, especially *The Waste Land* and quatrain poems like *Sweeney Erect*. In this respect Eliot is unmitigatedly anti-romantic whereas Gay is not.

Certainly Macheath's song towards the end of the 'Dance a la ronde in the French Manner', with the whores providing a chorus, Air XXII, 'Youth's the Season made for Joys', conveys a virtually heroic determination to live life to the full in the face of time the destroyer and the ultimate reality of death, especially as he is on the run and even more under the shadow of the gallows than usual. This song is a variation on the theme of *carpe diem* (enjoy the day) or 'Gather ye rosebuds while ye may', popular with Elizabethan and Cavalier poets, and Macheath, insisting that 'Love is then our Duty', shares the defiant confidence of the speaker in Marvell's 'To His Coy Mistress' rather than the inert defeatism of Eliot's J. Alfred Prufrock. Yet despite the almost ritualistic jollity of the first stanza, there is a hint of poignancy in the words 'While we may' in the concluding lines: 'Let's be gay, / While we may, / Beauty's a Flower, despis'd in decay.' And this poignancy becomes much more pronounced in the second stanza, which opens, 'Let us drink and sport to-day, / Ours is not to-morrow.' Time is never on the side of youth ('Love with Youth flies swift away'), but since Macheath's days seem to be strictly numbered, 'Ours is not to-morrow' could well be literally true in his case. If he does not 'drink and sport to-day', he may never do so. Only the reprieve at the end of the play prevents his immediate execution. Macheath's song is therefore a romantic gesture in a very unromantic world, a courageous plea for life against death that unsentimentally recognizes the inevitable victory of death sooner or later, 'sooner' being the relevant word in this context: 'Dance and sing, / Time's on the Wing, / Life never knows the return of Spring.' Superficially, Macheath's short-lived revelry with the whores is anti-romantic, but it transcends burlesque to become part of Gay's low-life romance.

The core of this low-life romance is, however, to be found in Macheath's relationships with Polly and Lucy and is closely connected with the theme of marriage. Polly and Lucy are alone in the play in thinking romantically about marriage, and given the world they inhabit it is a considerable achievement to hold a romantic conception of marriage at all, let alone to cling to it so steadfastly. The aim of each girl is to be recognized as Macheath's true wife, and according to Macheath's final speech, in which he tells Polly that 'we were really marry'd' (III.XVII), it is she who has acquired this status, although he characteristically adds that she should keep this secret for the time being. What in romance would be an occasion for general satisfaction and even rejoicing has to be suppressed for fear of offending Polly's many rivals. As a conclusion to a low-life romance, Macheath's final song, Air LXIX, 'Thus I stand like the Turk, with his Doxies around', is appropriately ambiguous. The line, 'Though willing to all; with but one he retires', might suggest that though still theoretically 'willing to all' he now resists temptation and will remain true to the 'one he retires' with—Polly. But the echo of Air XXIII, in which 'The Cock by Hens attended' eventually singles 'One . . . from the Crew', the nagging insistence on his extreme vulnerability to women ('his Passion confound . . . his Inconstancy burns . . . subdue him

. . . provoke his Desires'), and the sustained simile of that far from monogamous institution, the harem, remind us that he earlier confesses to loving 'the Sex' and that he may well remain 'willing to all' in a very practical sense. He has, after all, shown no signs of being sexually constrained by his marriage to Polly, to judge from his continuing involvement with whores after their wedding.

Macheath obviously revels in being 'like the Turk, with his Doxies around', and his scant regard for marriage is most fully symbolized in another scene in which he is surrounded by women, that in the condemned cell when six 'wives' come to take their leave of him. One of the most famous witticisms in the play occurs in Macheath's soliloquy after his arrest when he is wondering what to say to the pregnant Lucy:

> But I promis'd the Wench Marriage.—What signifies a Promise to a Woman? Does not Man in Marriage itself promise a hundred things that he never means to perform? Do all we can, Women will believe us; for they look upon a Promise as an Excuse for following their own Inclinations. (II.viii)

Yet incisive as these quips are, they seem like schoolboyish irreverence compared with the thoroughly jaundiced attitude to marriage shared by Lockit and the Peachums. Macheath clearly regards wedding vows as part of a ceremonial charade one should not take too seriously, and with that throwaway phrase, 'Do all we can', he puts the blame on women for not playing the game by his lighthearted rules, for treating the whole business of marriage with a solemnity it does not deserve. Upbraided by Lucy in the next scene for deceiving her and making her pregnant, he speaks of himself as her husband, and when she expresses surprise at what she regards as an audacious lie, he attempts to reassure her by explaining his somewhat unorthodox interpretation of the word:

> In ev'ry respect but the Form, and that, my Dear, may be said over us at any time.—Friends should not insist upon Ceremonies. From a Man of Honour, his Word is as good as his Bond. (II.ix)

The language has the formality of romance, but the situation of a promiscuous rogue trying to pacify a pregnant mistress is positively picaresque. The burlesque of romance could not be more clear, especially as Lucy replies in an equally formal way, ''Tis the Pleasure of all you fine Men to insult the Women you have ruin'd,' apparently accepting him at his own evaluation of himself as a kind of aristocrat.

Nevertheless, the burlesque cannot disguise the way in which

Macheath genuinely does propose to rescue a damsel in distress (low-life damsel, low-life distress) even though he is at the same time extricating himself from an embarrassing situation. Considering that he lies to Lucy about the intimacy of his relationship with Polly, it would be easy to dismiss his subsequent promise as a totally insincere ploy, especially as the sceptical Lucy herself does; but in spite of the fact that he is, in some sense, married to Polly and that he would not be in prison but for that marriage, his remarks are not altogether dishonest and deceitful:

> Macheath To convince you of my Sincerity, if we can find the
>   Ordinary [the Chaplain of Newgate], I shall have no
>   Scruples of making you my Wife; and I know the
>   consequence of having two at a time.
> Lucy   That you are only to be hang'd, and so get rid of them both.
> Macheath I am ready, my dear Lucy, to give you satisfaction—if you
>   think there is any in Marriage.—What can a Man of
>   Honour say more?
>   (II.ix)

He does, for example, make it clear that for himself there can be no satisfaction in marriage, but that he is prepared to go through the formalities to give her peace of mind. This is certainly not all that one would expect from 'a Man of Honour', not in the world of romance anyway, but it is not dishonourable either. Fortunately for him, Lucy cannot find the Ordinary so he is not put to the test, but if she had returned with the Ordinary, it is hard to imagine Macheath avoiding the walk to the altar. There is, then, a kind of sincerity in Macheath's words—as much as he can afford in his unenviable position. Given his earlier mockery of the marriage ceremony, he is not simply being devious when he tries to convince Lucy that 'I shall have no Scruples of making you my Wife'. Since he can hardly have scruples about something he does not take seriously, he probably means exactly what he says. His reference to the punishment for bigamy ('I know the consequence of having two at a time'), which is intended to calm Lucy's fears by suggesting that he is not married to Polly, may appear to be pure duplicity. But coming from a professional criminal who more or less accepts that he will end up with a noose around his neck for one offence or another and who has even been admitting to himself that his days are strictly numbered, it is no more than an empty gesture, and an almost transparently ingenuous one, as Lucy's response, with its deeply ironic 'only', confirms. Macheath knows 'the consequence of having two at a time', but it cannot possibly be a deterrent in his case. If he is 'only to be hang'd', he might as well be hanged for a sheep *and* a lamb, for bigamy or polygamy *and* highway robbery. Lucy's remark about Macheath being able to 'get rid of' his wives is also ironic, because he will achieve this not, as one would expect, by killing them but by dying himself. She is implying that death is the easy way out for him, something he is only too willing to acknowledge when six of his 'wives' join him in the condemned cell. Far removed from the romance world as all this is, it is more than burlesque, Gay's treatment again being subtly ambiguous. Macheath behaves neither as a romance hero nor as a villain, neither as an idealized lover nor as a vile seducer. He emerges as a paradoxical blend of these opposites, as a figure of low-life romance. He would have preferred to have avoided Lucy, but since he cannot, he attempts to play 'the Man of Honour' to the best of his necessarily limited ability.

Because Lucy does not appear until halfway through the play, it is easy to relegate her to a subordinate role, but she is a more complex character than she may seem at first sight. Her stormy entry into the action in II.ix as an unmarried mother-to-be launching a broadside against her lover immediately distinguishes her from the more innocent and romantic Polly, and she can be played as an essentially comic character. It is possible to treat her jealous rage, her bitter animosity towards Polly culminating in her melodramatic attempt to murder her rival, and even her pregnant shape ('See here . . . how I am forc'd to bear about the load of Infamy you have laid upon me' (II.ix)) simply as sources of laughter, but this is as much a distortion of her as is the opposite tendency to treat her too seriously. She then becomes a pathetic victim of male sexuality and duplicity, driven to extremes by her desperate longing for and attempt to secure the moral justice she believes is her due—'I long to be made an honest Woman' (II.ix). If Gay had intended Lucy to be primarily comic, he would not have given her such manifestly sincere expressions of devotion to her lover as, 'What Love or Money can do shall be done: for all my Comfort depends upon your Safety', when Macheath asks her to help him escape from Newgate in II.xii, or 'Come then, my dear Husband—owe thy Life to me—and though you love me not—be grateful', just before she actually frees him in II.xv. Especially in the closing scene of Act II, in which she sings her most moving solo, Air XL, 'I like the Fox shall grieve', Lucy displays genuine tenderness and affection; her feelings are all the more remarkable in the light of the preceding comic confrontation between herself, Polly, and Macheath in II.xiii, during which she expresses the desire to act as hangman at Macheath's execution ('When you come to the Tree, should the Hangman refuse, /

These Fingers, with Pleasure, could fasten the Noose'). The pathos of Lucy's situation also emerges from her encounters with her callous father, who is completely indifferent to her feelings and to her appeals to him to spare Macheath's life, as in Airs XXXI, 'Is then his Fate decreed, Sir?', and LV, 'When he holds up his Hand arraign'd for his Life'. Lockit tells her:

> Learn to bear your Husband's Death like a reasonable Woman. 'Tis not the fashion, now-a-days, so much as to affect Sorrow upon these Occasions. No Woman would ever marry, if she had not the Chance of Mortality for a Release. . . . So, I think, you must ev'n do like other Widows—Buy your self Weeds, and be cheerful.   (II.xi)

Her actual freeing of Macheath from Newgate is therefore in total defiance of her father and is the most practical demonstration of her love for Macheath—'When a Woman loves; a kind Look, a tender Word can persuade her to any thing' (III.i). Lucy may admit to her father that love 'is a Misfortune that may happen to the most discreet Woman, and in Love we are all Fools alike' (III.i), but her behaviour continues to be controlled by her passion for Macheath.

Yet if Gay had intended Lucy to be primarily a figure of pathos, he would not have involved her so much in his burlesque of Italian opera and other comic aspects of the play. Above all, he would not have dissolved her predicament so completely in the general merrymaking of the finale. Viewed realistically, Lucy's plight is pathetic since she has apparently lost her battle with Polly for Macheath and must remain an unmarried mother-to-be, but Gay quite rightly does not draw any attention to this because the dénouement is deliberately artificial and non-realistic. Lucy, like Macheath's other 'wives', joins in the song and dance with which the play ends following Macheath's plea to 'give this Day to Mirth' (III.xvii). In his treatment of Lucy, Gay achieves a fine balance between comedy and pathos that seems entirely appropriate for a low-life romance, 'a Newgate pastoral'. The comedy and burlesque prevent the pathos from coming too much to the fore, and conversely the pathos prevents the comedy from becoming purely burlesque or from degenerating into farce.

Polly, who remains head-over-heels in love with Macheath throughout the play, even after his attempt to 'disown her' in II.xiii, is a more obviously romantic figure than Lucy, but Gay's treatment of her is certainly not lacking in the ambivalence which characterizes his portrayal of Lucy. This is not surprising considering that their fates become very closely interwoven—Lucy actually says: 'Then our Cases,

my dear Polly, are exactly alike. Both of us indeed have been too fond'
(III.viii)—and given the fact that after II.xii they are usually on stage
together. The resemblance between them is most explicit in the stylized
symmetry of III.xi, in which both girls first address the rearrested
Macheath and then plead with their respective fathers to show clemency.
Polly encounters exactly the same cynicism about love and marriage
from her parents as Lucy does from her father. For Peachum, a pretty,
reliable girl like his daughter is an important business asset because her
sexuality can be advantageously exploited. When Mrs Peachum
expresses alarm in case 'Polly should be in love' (I.iv), as though that
would be tantamount to contracting a grave illness, her equally
concerned husband declares that 'A handsome Wench in our way of
Business is as profitable as at the Bar of a Temple Coffee-House, who
looks upon it as her Livelihood to grant every Liberty but one'. A little
later he tells Polly herself:

> I am not against your toying and trifling with a Customer in the way of
> Business, or to get out a Secret, or so. But if I find out that you have
> play'd the fool and are married, you Jade you, I'll cut your Throat,
> Hussy.   (I.VII)

Considering that he himself treats Polly as 'a Property', it is ironic that he
should complain so bitterly about the possibility of his daughter marrying
and consequently becoming her husband's 'Property': 'Married! If the
Wench does not know her own Profit, sure she knows her own Pleasure
better than to make herself a Property!' (I.iv).

The Peachums are, of course, furious when they learn that Polly has
actually married Macheath, and Polly's declaration that she 'did not
marry him (as 'tis the Fashion) cooly and deliberately for Honour or
Money' but because 'I love him' (I.viii) does nothing to improve matters.
Mrs Peachum's remarks immediately before she faints from shock at the
news, 'Love him! worse and worse! I thought the Girl had been better
bred', treat love as a breach of social etiquette, and in I.x she puts it more
strongly, making out that love is not only contemptible but unfeminine
as well: 'What, is the Fool in Love in earnest then? I hate thee for being
particular: Why, Wench, thou art a Shame to thy very Sex.' Both
Peachum and his wife clearly regard Polly's marriage as a supreme act of
folly and even a form of lunacy. Peachum's rhetorical question to Polly,
'Do you think your Mother and I should have liv'd comfortably so long
together, if ever we had been married?' (I.viii), leads almost inevitably to
his strangely-phrased real question to her, 'are you ruin'd or no?', in

which he equates 'ruin'd' with 'married', thus inverting the usual sense of 'ruin'd' in such a context. A girl who lost her virginity before marriage and therefore damaged her marriage prospects would normally have been thought to be 'ruin'd' and to have committed a supreme act of folly. Mrs Peachum also speaks of Polly's 'Ruin', blaming it mainly on the romantic illusions nourished by 'Those cursed Play-books she reads' (i.x). According to Mrs Peachum, it would have been much better for Polly to have had an affair with Macheath than to have married him—''Tis Marriage, Husband, that makes it a Blemish' (i.ix). It is exceedingly ironic that among Polly's reasons for marrying Macheath are the wish to avoid being 'ruin'd' by him and the concomitant wish to avoid causing her parents any distress:

> When he kist me so closely he prest,
>   'Twas so sweet that I must have comply'd:
> So I thought it both safest and best
>   To marry, for fear you should chide.

(Air VIII)

The two songs in i.viii in which Polly expresses and justifies her love for Macheath, Airs VIII and X, do not have the desired effect on her parents, although by the end of the scene Polly mistakenly believes that she has reconciled them to her marriage and that 'all my Sorrows are at an end'. In fact, her sorrows begin in earnest shortly after this hopeful assertion when she discovers her parents' intentions in i.x. To protect their own interests and to acquire the proceeds of Macheath's lucrative highway robberies, their plan is for Polly to 'Secure what he hath got' and then to have him 'peach'd' (brought to trial by providing evidence against him on criminal charges) and executed. From the Peachums' point of view, this is good business sense, but they also think they are doing their daughter a service in ridding her of the encumbrance of a husband. 'And had not you the common Views of a Gentlewoman in your Marriage, Polly?', asks her father, meaning the arranging 'Of a Jointure, and of being a Widow' (a jointure was a legal agreement for the joint-holding of property by a married couple to ensure that the wife was provided for if widowed). Polly is shocked at these proposals, especially as she is expected to help in putting them into effect ('But your Duty to your Parents, Hussy, obliges you to hang him', her mother tells her), and cannot contemplate the prospect of being parted from Macheath; yet her father contends that it is this prospect and this alone that justifies the institution of marriage, particularly for a woman:

Why, that is the whole Scheme and Intention of all Marriage Articles. The comfortable Estate of Widow-hood, is the only Hope that keeps up a Wife's Spirits. Where is the Woman who would scruple to be a Wife, if she had it in her Power to be a Widow whenever she pleas'd?

What is 'not so very unreasonable' for Peachum is intolerable and unthinkable to Polly because it amounts to murdering the man she loves. Peachum, with his no-nonsense, 'every Man in his Business' approach to such issues, cannot understand his daughter's talk of murder. For him, 'there is no Malice in the Case' since as a thief-taker it is his job to arrest thieves like Macheath, just as it is Macheath's 'Employment to rob'. Peachum even believes that Macheath would prefer to be peached by his wife and parents-in-law than by someone outside the family: 'Since the thing sooner or later must happen, I dare say, the Captain himself would like that we should get the Reward for his Death sooner than a Stranger.'

Because of her belief in love and her total commitment to Macheath in the face of such parental callousness and cynicism, Polly may appear to be more naïve and innocent than she really is. In the largely unromantic world of the play, especially that of Lockit and the Peachums, Polly does emerge as a romantic heroine, being the one character who is more or less unscathed by her environment. She is the nearest thing to an embodiment of virtue in a milieu dominated by self-interest and greed, and in matters of love she is ingenuous enough to mistake her promiscuous rogue of a husband for a romance hero faithful unto death—'I have no Reason to doubt you, for I find in the Romance you lent me, none of the great Heroes were ever false in Love' (I.xiii). Nevertheless, Polly herself belongs to that milieu. If she is a romantic heroine, she is also a low-life character. On discovering Polly's marriage, her mother warns her that she will be 'as ill-us'd, and as much neglected, as if thou hadst married a Lord!' (I.viii), but Polly is in love with a highwayman, not an aristocrat, and she is a considerable help to her father in his criminal business dealings. When she tells Peachum, 'A Woman knows how to be mercenary, though she hath never been in a Court or at an Assembly' and 'A Girl who cannot grant some Things, and refuse what is most material, will make but a poor hand of her Beauty, and soon be thrown upon the Common' (I.vii), she is saying what she knows will please him, but she is also revealing her intimate knowledge of the ways of the world and the underworld. Furthermore, she is not the impractical and helpless milksop that 'romantic heroine' may suggest. Polly possesses a will of her own: 'I know as well as any of the fine Ladies how to make the most of my self

THE BEGGAR'S OPERA AS ROMANCE AND ANTI-ROMANCE

and of my Man too' (I.vii). She marries Macheath without her parents'
approval and tries to keep this a secret, but when they learn the truth she
is sufficiently tough and resilient to stand up to their attack and to defend
herself and her marriage.

There are other ways, including her part in the operatic burlesque, in
which Gay prevents Polly's romantic aura from becoming dis-
proportionate. Even in some of her most poignant scenes, there are
undercurrents of burlesque and comedy that counteract any tendency
towards sentimentality without damaging the poignancy. Her soliloquy
in I.xii, in which she imagines Macheath being taken to the gallows at
Tyburn, is her anguished response to her parents' decision to capture and
prosecute her husband:

> I hear the Crowd extolling his Resolution and Intrepidity!—What
> Vollies of Sighs are sent from the Windows of Holborn, that so comely
> a Youth should be brought to disgrace!—I see him at the Tree! The
> whole Circle are in Tears!—even Butchers weep!

While expressive of her fears, the rhetoric borders on the comic because
of the apparent discrepancy between what is being spoken about, the
public execution of a common criminal, and the elevated way in which it
is described. The passage could almost be a burlesque of the overwrought
and self-indulgent agonizings of tragic heroines in the 'sentimental'
drama of the period, but Gay redeems such rhetoric by making it a
genuine vehicle for Polly's emotions.

The following scene, the most tender encounter between Polly and
Macheath in the play, exhibits a very similar ambivalence. While it is not
inappropriate for Macheath's declaration of everlasting love, 'May my
Pistols miss Fire, and my Mare slip her Shoulder while I am pursu'd, if I
ever forsake thee!', to be made in terms of his profession as a
highwayman, there is nevertheless a burlesque incongruity between his
grandiloquence and his swearing by the tools of his criminal trade. And
with Polly acting the part of a romance heroine to Macheath's romance
hero, this incongruity is sustained throughout the scene. When Polly
asks, 'you could not leave me behind you—could you?', she speaks with
the intensity of a sentimental heroine, but the context she imagines,
'Were you sentenc'd to Transportation', brings the factitious intensity of
sentimental drama and romance down to earth with a bump without
invalidating the depth of her feelings. What rescues the ultra-heroic
rhetoric of Macheath's reply, 'Is there any Power, any Force that could
tear me from thee? . . . But to tear me from thee is impossible!', from

being purely burlesque is the incisive social satire directed against the greed, vanity, and folly of the well-to-do that is sandwiched between these pledges of eternal devotion: 'You might sooner tear a Pension out of the Hands of a Courtier, a Fee from a Lawyer, a pretty Woman from a Looking-glass, or any Woman from Quadrille' (*the* fashionable card-game at the time). The sudden transition from the abstract ('any Power, any Force') to the mundane helps to undermine the heroic posturings of romance characters, yet paradoxically makes Macheath's rhetoric more credible than it would otherwise have been since he is referring to the world he knows, not to some cloud-cuckoo land of impossible ideals. The parting of the two lovers, precipitated by Macheath's need to flee from the Peachums, is also on the brink of burlesque but transcends it. Polly's moist-eyed, 'But oh!—how shall I speak it? I must be torn from thee. We must part', leads on to her equally tearful, 'One Kiss and then—one Kiss—begone—farewell', and Macheath's even more exclamatory, 'My Hand, my Heart, my Dear, is so rivited to thine, that I cannot unloose my Hold.' Tear-jerking separation scenes with hero and heroine insisting on the impossibility of parting were commonplace in contemporary tragedy, and Gay certainly has one eye on these, but he again redeems the language and the situation to achieve true pathos, although it is pathos on the edge of comedy.

There are some splendid examples of this ambivalence near the end of Act II. Polly's first words on arriving at Newgate to visit Macheath are: 'Where is my dear Husband?—Was a Rope ever intended for this Neck!—O let me throw my Arms about it, and throttle thee with Love!' (II.xiii). To a man with little hope of avoiding death by hanging, Polly's use of 'throttle' is neither tactful nor reassuring, although she employs this hyperbole to convey the force and quality of her love. We may be amused by 'throttle' but we nonetheless accept her words as sincere and heartfelt. In II.xiv when Peachum arrives angrily to take his daughter home, Polly appeals to Macheath, who is wearing prisoner's chains, to 'twist thy Fetters about me, that he may not haul me from thee'. Taken literally, her demand to be entangled in Macheath's chains so that she cannot be separated from him seems exaggerated and rather comical, but at the same time the exaggeration does convey the desperation she feels. The same paradoxical blend of the serious and the comical occurs in Air XXXIX, 'No Power on Earth can e'er divide', in which Polly sings about 'The Knot that Sacred Love hath ty'd' during a tug-of-war involving her husband, her father, and herself; while she clings to Macheath, Peachum tries to drag her away from him. What is particularly interesting is that

Polly's metaphorical language, 'When Parents draw against our Mind, / The True-love's Knot they faster bind', applies quite literally to the comic action since, by pulling his daughter, Peachum is likely to bind Polly and Macheath more closely together in his chains, which therefore become 'The True-love's Knot'. The comic undertow in the song certainly does not cancel out Polly's passionate solemnity, but it does qualify it, again preventing any sentimentality. In all these instances, romance and anti-romance go hand in hand as befits a low-life romance, but in attempting this extraordinary fusion of pathos and comedy, Gay is walking a tightrope over Niagara. That he succeeds in keeping his balance at all, let alone so well, is an artistic near-miracle.

4 The Beggar's Opera *as Satire*

'The World is all alike'

One of the most important features of Gay's ironic method of burlesque, as opposed to the more usual method of comic exaggeration, is that it readily lends itself to social and political satire. In pretending, through the mouthpiece of the Beggar, that his mock-opera about the underworld is a conventional opera, Gay is inverting Italian opera; this is the burlesque. Gay simultaneously inverts and burlesques the conventional romance. Yet in treating his low-life characters as though they were from high life, he is able to create a dimension that completely transcends burlesque. Compared with the idealized heroes and heroines of opera and romance, Gay's characters are all too human, but their very humanity makes them excellent weapons to deploy against the far from ideal high life of the real world. Many episodes in the play can therefore be interpreted in at least two ways, as operatic burlesque and as social satire; the one is indivisibly linked with the other. Gay is being extremely ironic when he makes Macheath speak of himself as a 'Man of Honour' or be called a 'Gentleman' and a 'great Man' as though he were an aristocratic hero from opera or romance, but the irony bounces back to raise doubts about those who do regard themselves as 'men of honour' or are called 'gentlemen' and 'great men' in real life. Alexander the Great may make an impressive operatic hero, but what exactly did his 'greatness' consist of? Wisdom and charity? Or brutality and repression on a grand scale? Gay's burlesque of operas like *Alessandro* becomes a way of asking awkward questions about the world. In fact, are courtiers and aristocrats, politicians and military leaders, doctors and lawyers, any better than common criminals like Macheath?

This is the issue that Gay poses throughout the play by treating highwaymen ('Gentlemen of the Road') as honourable gentlemen, and the answer given by the Beggar himself in III.xvi, after the Player has intervened to urge him to provide a happy operatic ending, is in the negative: 'Through the whole Piece you may observe such a similitude of Manners in high and low Life, that it is difficult to determine whether (in the fashionable Vices) the fine Gentlemen imitate the Gentlemen of the Road, or the Gentlemen of the Road the fine Gentlemen.' But the Beggar goes even further when he explains that his original intention to do 'strict poetical Justice', with Macheath hanged and the other characters destined for the gallows or transportation, 'would have carried a most excellent Moral'. This 'Moral', calmly expounded by the Beggar as though it were a commonplace, turns out on inspection to be daringly outrageous: ' "Twould have shown that the lower Sort of People have their Vices in a degree as well as the Rich: And that they are punish'd for them.' The Beggar implies that, whereas the vices of the upper classes are so well known as not to need pointing out, he is drawing attention to the less obvious fact that 'the lower Sort of People', such as criminals and prostitutes, also have vices. This ironic reversal of conventional social prejudices and valuations is a witty but devastating indictment of 'the Rich', who are implicitly blamed for setting the lower classes a bad example and so for being ultimately responsible for others' vices as well as their own. It is therefore a terrible perversion of natural justice that only 'the lower Sort of People' are punished for their vices, since those who should be punished, 'the Rich', succeed in evading the force of the law. In the eyes of the world, only one of 'the lower Sort of People' can be a criminal or prostitute. A man or woman who is one of 'the Rich' or who rises in the world to become one of 'the Rich' is not seen as a criminal or prostitute, regardless of his or her conduct. 'Money', Peachum tells his wife, 'is the true Fuller's Earth for Reputations, there is not a Spot or a Stain but what it can take out' ('Fuller's Earth' was used in the fulling process to clean and reinforce fabrics). 'A rich Rogue now-a-days is fit Company for any Gentleman' (I.ix).

In the condemned cell, Macheath ponders on the issue of crime and punishment, wondering why, since the law should apply to the whole of society and not just the poorest and least respectable section of it, 'we han't better Company, / Upon Tyburn Tree!' (Air LXVII). The answer, recalling Peachum's remark to his wife, is that 'Gold from Law can take out the Sting'; but having identified bribery and corruption as the main explanation, Macheath goes on to suggest that it would be difficult to apply the law rigorously to the aristocracy and the bourgeoisie because it would amount to a policy of genocide: 'if rich Men like us were to swing, / 'Twou'd thin the Land, such Numbers to string / Upon Tyburn Tree!' It is the extent of corruption in high places that Lockit wittily draws attention to in Air XXX, 'When you censure the Age', in which he advises Peachum to be careful in voicing criticism of their social superiors for fear of offending all and sundry: 'If you mention Vice or Bribe, / 'Tis so pat to all the Tribe; / Each crys—That was levell'd at me.' Peachum has just been commenting on the ability of the well-to-do to escape legal punishment—'Can it be expected that we should hang our Acquaintance for nothing, when our Betters will hardly save theirs without being paid for it' (II.x)—something he does more forcefully in I.iv. Explaining to his wife that 'Murder is as fashionable a Crime as a Man can be guilty of', he informs her that the 'many fine Gentlemen' charged with murder usually have 'wherewithal to persuade the Jury to bring it in Manslaughter', thus escaping the mandatory death penalty meted out to lesser mortals.

Macheath and his gang of highway-robbers, whom Gay ironically likens to a group of aristocrats, repeatedly express their conviction that high society is more corrupt than the underworld. When Matt of the Mint proposes robbing a gambler who 'is never without Money', Macheath quickly rejects the idea, pointing out that 'He's a good honest kind of a Fellow, and one of us', meaning a fellow-robber (III.iv). Goodness and honesty are paradoxically associated with criminals rather than with their 'betters', who are implicitly accused of being even bigger robbers than professional thieves. Lawyers, for example, are equated with professional gamblers in Air XXIV, 'The Gamesters and Lawyers are Jugglers alike', and with thieves in Air XI, 'A Fox may steal your Hens, Sir'; but whereas a thief may steal 'your Goods and Plate', a lawyer will not be content with less than 'your whole Estate'. Gay himself is not actually endorsing the view that criminals are more trustworthy and reliable than people in political, professional, and public life, but he is saying that appearances are often very deceptive and that those who pass in society as good and honest may in fact be anything but. At least you know where you stand with honest-to-goodness criminals, but since respectability and hypocrisy often go hand in hand, it is much more difficult to know where you are with respectable 'criminals' such as courtiers, politicians, lawyers, and businessmen. When Gay was writing, bribery was endemic in court circles and political life, and corrupt practices were carried on with impunity, but his point is that such behaviour, however widespread, is no different morally from the misdeeds of criminals. Indeed, it is less excusable, partly because high society should be setting standards, not abusing them, and partly because of the hypocrisy involved, the deceitful attempts to cover up morally reprehensible conduct or even to present it as honourable and virtuous. Taken relatively rather than absolutely, Macheath's labelling of his fellow-thief as good and honest, while superficially absurd, carries a kind of truth.

As an alternative to robbing the 'good honest kind of a Fellow', Macheath suggests 'the Money-lenders', who lent cash at exorbitantly high interest rates, as more appropriate targets. 'I hate Extortion', declares Macheath, and although coming from a highwayman this may seem the height of hypocrisy, it paradoxically acquires considerable moral force. Macheath is really accusing the money-lenders of two things: theft and usury. Money-lenders may not have been particularly reputable, but they were not regarded as criminals. Yet in exploiting situations for financial gain, is their behaviour morally superior to that of criminals? Is money-lending at extortionate rates significantly different from robbery? If not, why is one form of robbery socially acceptable and another not? And what sort of a topsy-turvy world is it that countenances such alarming discrepancies? Furthermore, the charge of 'Extortion' carries with it the charge of usury and covetousness, sins that could not be attributed to Macheath, who is a reckless spendthrift, not a miser. Macheath's generosity to the ladies of the town, attested to by Mrs Trapes in III.vi, is evident in the tavern scene, but he is no less generous to his male associates. When he joins his gang in II.ii, one of the questions he asks is, 'In the Divison of our Booty, have I ever shown the least Marks of Avarice or Injustice?', and there is no suggestion that he has. It is very significant that just before he speaks of the money-lenders, he provides with cash two members of his gang, Ben Budge and Matt of the Mint, saying, 'When my Friends are in Difficulties, I am always glad that my Fortune can be serviceable to them.' Macheath actually earns the right to say, 'I hate Extortion'. His liberality leads Ben to lament that 'so generous a Man' as Macheath is 'involv'd in such Difficulties, as oblige him to live with such ill Company, and herd with Gamesters', and since, according to Matt, 'many of the Quality are of the Profession', the 'ill Company' is identified with the upper classes. A kind-hearted highwayman who mixes with 'the Quality' runs a great risk of being corrupted by them, a point made in I.iv by Mrs Peachum when she says of Macheath: 'What business hath he to keep Company with Lords and Gentlemen? he should leave them to prey upon one another.' In the same scene, Peachum remarks on Macheath's weakness for gambling even though he loses regularly, 'The Man that proposes to get Money by Play should have the Education of a fine Gentleman, and be train'd up to it from his Youth'; the implication is that Macheath is totally out of his depth with such poker-faced cheats as 'fine Gentlemen' and cannot hope to win. In III.iv, Matt too comments on the absurdity of a world in which the lowest form of humanity, gamblers, are 'admitted amongst the politest Company', while highwaymen are treated with contempt and relegated to the lowest stratum of society. In wondering why 'we are not more respected', Matt is drawing attention to the fact that social status has no relation to moral qualities. If upper-class gamblers are respected, there is no reason on moral grounds why lower-class highwaymen should not be at least equally respected. 'Why are the Laws levell'd at us?', asks another member of the gang, Jemmy Twitcher, in II.i, 'are we more dishonest than the rest of Mankind?'; Gay's implied answer is 'no', although this does not mean that he regards them as less dishonest either.

The parallel between what the Beggar calls 'fine Gentlemen' and 'Gentlemen of the Road' is most fully developed in II.i–ii, the only occasion on which Macheath's gang is assembled on stage. Matt of the Mint makes the comparison explicit when he exclaims, 'Show me a Gang of Courtiers that can say as much', after several members of the gang have acknowledged their total commitment to their collective enterprise with assertions of their positive qualities. They are 'above the Fear of Death' (Crook-finger'd Jack), 'Sound Men, and true' (Wat Dreary), and 'Of try'd Courage, and indefatigable Industry' (Robin of Bagshot). They could easily be mistaken for dedicated professional soldiers, and the issue pervading the play of whether there is any significant difference between the activities of the gang and those of the army is raised by Jemmy Twitcher: 'What we win, Gentlemen, is our own by the Law of Arms, and the Right of Conquest.' Such military clichés are radically undermined by being placed in the mouth of a highwayman. Macheath, who is called 'Captain' throughout the play, 'looks upon himself in the Military Capacity, as a Gentleman by his Profession', as Peachum points out in I.viii; he himself speaks of highwaymen and 'the other Gentlemen of the Sword' (army officers) in the same breath in II.iii when claiming that he has been as responsible as 'any Recruiting Officer in the Army' for providing London with 'free-hearted Ladies'. Yet Macheath's exemplary treatment of his men would put to shame many of those who prided themselves on being officers and gentlemen, assuming that they could feel shame. Two members of the gang, Ben Budge and Matt of the Mint, go so far as to defend their 'military' activities on idealistic grounds in II.i. Ben, giving voice to a democratic and egalitarian ideology, argues that 'We are for a just Partition of the World', and Matt makes a similar claim in presenting Macheath's gang as a modern version of Robin Hood and his Merry Men who 'retrench the Superfluities of Mankind'. Matt is again insisting that the values of society are upside down. Beginning with the assertion that 'The World is avaritious, and I hate Avarice', which incidentally foreshadows Macheath's 'I hate Extortion', Matt contends that it is the miserly and the covetous, not thieves and highwaymen, who are the real 'Robbers of Mankind, for Money was made for the Free-hearted and Generous, and where is the Injury of taking from another, what he hath not the Heart to make use of?' The incongruity between the speakers themselves and their chivalric sentiments and mannered rhetoric burlesques all those honourable pledges couched in superlatives that spring so readily from the lips of characters in Italian opera and contemporary tragedy. But Gay simultaneously suggests that it is less incongruous for Macheath's gang to speak of truth, courage, loyalty, and justice than it is for 'a Gang of Courtiers' or politicians or army officers or any other social group who do so in real life.

Nevertheless, Gay does not make the mistake of overromanticizing Macheath and the gang by accepting them at their own idealistic estimate of themselves. To some extent this is because they function throughout at a burlesque level, but equally important is the fact that their actions do not always accord with their words. Although Matt's use of 'say' rather than 'do' when he asks to be shown 'a Gang of Courtiers that can say as much' is natural enough in the context, it brings to mind the possibility that the gang's behaviour will not always be up to expectation. In the condemned cell, Macheath is far from being 'above the Fear of Death' and needs a constant supply of drink to put on a brave front. Even more important is the revelation in III.xiv that Jemmy Twitcher has peached Macheath, presumably by providing evidence against him at his trial. Jemmy drives a coach and horses through the confident assumption that no member of the gang would ever peach one of the others, as expressed in Nimming Ned's and Harry Padington's ringing rhetorical questions in

II.i, 'Who is there here that would not dye for his Friend?' and 'Who is there here that would betray him for his Interest?' Yet Gay makes even Jemmy's Judas-like act of betrayal further his satire on high society. Surprisingly enough, Macheath is philosophical rather than furious, accepting with resignation 'that the World is all alike, and that even our Gang can no more trust one another than other People' (III.xiv). He had taken it for granted that there is very little honesty and loyalty in the world, but had believed that his gang, who 'have still Honour enough to break through the Corruptions of the World' (III.iv), would remain a beacon of truth in the almost universal darkness of greed, self-seeking, and falsehood enveloping society. Unfortunately, the once high standards of the gang have plummeted. The word 'even' used in connection with 'our Gang' makes it clear that highwaymen, apparently the last hope for mankind, are now no better than their social superiors, but there is the further implication that this debasement actually stems from those superiors. Macheath makes this point more forcefully in Air XLIV, which opens, 'The Modes of the Court so common are grown, / That a true Friend can hardly be met.' The source of social degeneration is here pinpointed as the court itself, whose 'Modes' are spreading throughout the whole of society like pollution in a river, endangering the underworld itself. Macheath, however, remains untarnished in spite of associating with aristocrats, and in giving money to Ben Budge and Matt of the Mint he proves that he is 'not a meer Court Friend, who professes every thing and will do nothing' (III.iv). Even the much more corrupt Lockit seems to be suggesting in Air LVI, which opens, 'Our selves, like the Great, to secure a Retreat, / When Matters require it, must give up our Gang', that he has been contaminated by the 'great' world of the court and parliament. He excuses his and Peachum's plot against Macheath by arguing that in acting out of self-interest they are simply behaving 'like the Great', who have established numerous precedents for double-dealing and treachery.

If Macheath is a low-life equivalent of an aristocrat and an army officer, Lockit, as chief jailor of Newgate, is a low-life equivalent of a civil servant or bureaucrat. His superficially polite manner, resembling the façades adopted by officials in public life, hardly disguises his totally selfish nature. When the newly-arrested Macheath arrives at Newgate in II.vii, Lockit greets him with, 'Noble Captain, you are welcome', but in his next breath demands a bribe: 'You know the custom, Sir. Garnish, Captain, Garnish' (the 'Garnish' was the payment extorted from prisoners on entering jail). While maintaining his initial politeness with

'Sir' and 'Captain', he uses the threat of putting Macheath into the heaviest possible fetters to make him comply. Since eighteenth-century prisons were run on commercial lines, the system was open to tremendous abuse, and petty corruption was widespread. A man who was free with his money could live fairly comfortably in Newgate, but a poor man could not expect much mercy. As Macheath wittily observes: 'The Fees here are so many, and so exorbitant, that few Fortunes can bear the Expence of getting off handsomly, or of dying like a Gentleman.' When Macheath protests at being given heavy chains, Lockit offers him a range 'from one Guinea to ten', and after receiving his 'Garnish' he substitutes chains suitable for 'the nicest Man in England'. Gay is, of course, satirizing the small-scale racketeering which was rife in contemporary prisons, but more importantly he implies that what goes on in Newgate is no different from what goes on in the corridors of power at court and in Whitehall, except that the latter is on a much larger scale. He achieves this mainly by making Lockit speak in a hybrid way, using the language of the beau monde as well as that of Newgate. He speaks as a jailor when he makes a direct demand for the 'Garnish', but his subsequent request for a bribe is euphemistically phrased in the idiom of courtiers and politicians; 'uses me with Civility' is the polite equivalent for 'gives me a bribe' in 'When a Gentleman uses me with Civility, I always do the best I can to please him'. The incongruity of Lockit's eulogistic description of Macheath's chains, 'Never was better work.—How genteely they are made!—They will sit as easy as a Glove', more appropriate for exquisite, made-to-measure clothes, again closes the usual gap between the worlds of courtiers and criminals. And his hypothetical suggestion of having 'the best Gentleman in the Land in my Custody' does carry the implication that it is by no means unthinkable that such a person should be behind bars. Since 'best' as applied to gentlemen has more to do with modishness than with morality, 'the best Gentleman in the Land' may be more deserving of prison than Macheath.

In II.xii, Macheath himself makes the connection between the malpractices of Lockit and the conduct of civil servants and other officials. In thinking of ways to regain his freedom, Macheath, observing that Lockit's 'Perquisites for the Escape of Prisoners must amount to a considerable Sum in the Year', decides to try bribery as the most likely means of success. But it is not only in low life that 'Money well tim'd, and properly apply'd, will do any thing'. Macheath illustrates this principle in Air XXXIII, 'If you at an Office solicit your Due', showing the vulnerability of people as diverse as clerks and ladies to the

'Perquisite'—'That Reason with all is prevailing'. Contrary to appearances, neither high office nor middle-class respectability imply immunity from corruption. Lockits are everywhere, and how could it be any different when money not only makes this fallen world go round but has become the measure of all things?

Lockit's basic philosophy of eat or be eaten and of the survival of the least innocent is baldly stated in his scolding of Lucy in III.i and his soliloquy in the following scene. Furious with his daughter not so much for letting Macheath escape from Newgate as for doing so without obtaining a substantial bribe, or even a bribe at all, he repudiates her talk about love with his callous advice: 'If you would not be look'd upon as a Fool, you should never do any thing but upon the Foot of Interest.' Anyone acting out of generosity will be exploited, not thanked, and will be regarded with contempt, not gratitude. Lockit's view that to do anything except out of self-interest is the height of folly is based on his conception of human nature and society:

> Lions, Wolves, and Vulturs don't live together in Herds, Droves or Flocks.—Of all Animals of Prey, Man is the only sociable one. Every one of us preys upon his Neighbour, and yet we herd together. (III.ii)

Since all human beings are at bottom selfish and predatory, human society is ethically the same as a pike pond. This point is made explicit in the simile at the end of Air XLIII, 'Thus Gamesters united in Friendship are found', his song about the deceits of friendship: 'Like Pikes, lank with Hunger, who miss of their Ends, / They bite their Companions, and prey on their Friends.' Although gamblers illustrate Lockit's thesis particularly well, he sees gamblers as typical rather than exceptional. Trickery and deception are not the preserves of the underworld, but permeate all human transactions and relationships. Believing that his partner in organized crime, Peachum, is trying to out-wit him, he justifies his plan to-'over-reach' the man he calls 'my Companion, my Friend' by reference not to self-interest but to nothing less grandiose than 'the Custom of the World', which is equivalent to the law of the jungle: 'According to the Custom of the World, indeed, he may quote thousands of Precedents for cheating me—And shall not I make use of the Privilege of Friendship to make him a Return?' Peachum also upholds 'the Custom of the World' when accepting his wife's argument that, even though they like Macheath and owe much of their prosperity to him, they must proceed with their scheme to peach him to ensure their own safety: 'Then, indeed, we must comply with the Customs of the World, and make Gratitude give way to Interest' (I.xi). Starting from Lockit's premises, his argument in III.ii is sweetly reasonable and leads to his claim that, in ruthlessly pursuing their own ends, he and Peachum are merely behaving 'like honest Tradesmen'. Each of them is following the example of savage competitiveness and self-seeking expediency set by the business community, the rules of fair trade. In likening Peachum and himself to 'honest Tradesmen' and describing their power struggle as 'a fair Tryal', he is implying that they could conduct themselves in the even less humane way of dishonest tradesmen. Here Gay makes the activities of his low-life characters raise serious doubts not only about what goes on behind the scenes in the respectable world of business and commerce, but also about the ethical basis, or lack of one, of that world. Scenes like this make it very easy to understand why Bertolt Brecht was inspired to rewrite *The Beggar's Opera* in the 1920s as *Die Dreigroschenoper* (*The Threepenny Opera*) in order to communicate his Marxist belief that capitalism and criminality are two sides of the same coin.

That 'the World is all alike' is one of the points made in the scene between Lockit and Peachum where their well-maintained composure and usually intact façades momentarily break down to reveal their true selves (II.x). This is a mock-heroic version of the famous argument between Brutus and Cassius in *Julius Caesar*, the allusion to Shakespeare's characters pricking the bubble of self-importance in which Lockit and Peachum cocoon themselves; Lockit, for example, declaims, 'He that attacks my Honour, attacks my Livelyhood.' But the scene also refers to the real tussle going on at the time between Sir Robert Walpole and another powerful Whig politician, Lord Townshend, who was, in addition, Walpole's brother-in-law. Lockit and Peachum address each other as 'Brother' throughout the scene, but the significance of their hypocritical pretence to mutual respect and trust is not restricted to the two feuding politicians. Complaining bitterly about the slowness of the authorities in paying them their rewards for helping to secure the conviction and execution of criminals, Peachum threatens to withdraw his services to the state as a thief-taker: 'Unless the People in employment pay better, I promise them for the future, I shall let other Rogues live besides their own.' 'Rogues' are universal, but whereas low-life rogues are much more likely to die on the gallows than in their beds, upper-class rogues have nothing to fear since their position, their influence, and especially their money will always enable them to keep their good names as well as their necks intact. Lockit's subsequent complaint about the impertinence of 'the People in employment' for treating Peachum and himself 'with Contempt, as if our Profession were not reputable' carries even more serious allegations against the powers-that-be. By normal standards, Lockit and Peachum's activities as thief-takers, betraying their friends and acquaintances and sending them to almost certain death, are not in the least bit 'reputable' and could not possibly be called a 'Profession'. But the assumption behind Lockit's high-minded way of speaking about nefarious, underhand deals is that he and Peachum behave in much the same way as 'the People in employment' and members of the accredited professions, like law and politics, who are nevertheless regarded as 'reputable'. By the standards that prevail in high society, Lockit is convinced that he is 'reputable'; his only sin is not to belong to high society. To be 'reputable' has nothing to do with honesty and integrity, only with social status.

Although Peachum slightly qualifies Lockit's claim to be 'reputable', his words carry a sharp satirical sting: 'In one respect indeed, our Employment may be reckon'd dishonest, because, like Great Statesmen, we encourage those who betray their Friends.' Peachum does not actually admit to dishonesty, only that they 'may be reckon'd dishonest', and even then there is only 'one respect' in which they could possibly be accused of dishonesty. But that 'one respect' is sufficient to put 'great Statesmen' like Walpole and Lord Townshend in the dock. 'Great Statesmen' ought to provide an example to the nation and should not conduct their affairs like Peachum and Lockit; but since they do indulge in such deviousness as encouraging 'those who betray their Friends', they are morally indistinguishable from Peachum and Lockit. Of course, if the leaders of the nation are two-faced opportunists, their behaviour sets a pattern for others to follow and so ceases to be regarded as dishonest, which is why Peachum says that it 'may be reckon'd dishonest'— presumably by those old-fashioned enough to cling to something as outmoded as moral values.

The resemblance between great statesmen and Peachum and Lockit is sustained during the ensuing quarrel. Peachum's suggestion that Lockit has been guilty of 'a little unfair proceeding' meets the self-righteous retort: 'This is the first time my Honour was ever call'd in Question.' As indignation mounts on both sides and they seize each other by the throat, their language rapidly descends from such gentlemanly utterances to cruder but more honest ones, with Peachum saying, 'If I am hang'd, it shall be for ridding the World of an arrant Rascal', and Lockit replying, 'This Hand shall do the office of the Halter you deserve, and throttle you—you Dog!' At this point self-interest reasserts itself as they realize that they 'shall be both Losers in the Dispute', and the language of hypocrisy ('Brother, Brother') replaces the language of truth ('arrant Rascal' and 'you Dog'). ' 'Tis our mutual Interest', observes Peachum, referring to the need to patch up their differences, but when he continues, he speaks like a politician or national leader as though their argument is likely to have widespread repercussions such as war: ' 'tis for the Interest of the World we should agree.' By making Peachum and Lockit act the parts of great statesmen, Gay is suggesting that great statesmen themselves act their parts and that beneath their talk of honour they are really as motivated by self-interest as Peachum and Lockit.

In addition to his 'political' role, Peachum is the low-life equivalent of a prosperous member of the merchant class and is modelled on one of Gay's most infamous contemporaries, Jonathan Wild, who led a double life, one criminal and one apparently respectable. Wild actually was an underworld counterpart to a prosperous member of the merchant class. His trial in 1725 caused a sensation because of what it revealed about organized crime in London. On one side, he was a thief-taker who acted as a kind of policeman, arresting criminals (as Peachum does in II.v with the aid of constables) and arranging for evidence to be presented against them at their trials; 'And I'll prepare Matters for the Old-Baily', says Peachum in I.xi after deciding to peach Macheath. If the defendant were convicted, Wild would receive the statutory reward of forty pounds for his services, which was a not inconsiderable sum; Peachum refers to this in connection with Tom Gagg and Betty Sly in I.ii, and in II.x he agrees 'to go halves in Macheath' with Lockit. Thief-taking was therefore a lucrative business (Peachum talks about his 'Employment' being 'to take Robbers; every Man in his Business' in I.x) but it was a corrupt and corrupting one. For example, in persuading criminals to testify against their fellow-criminals, Wild frequently resorted to bribery, and Peachum presumably bribes Jemmy Twitcher to give evidence against Macheath. Wild's success as a thief-taker depended on his intimate knowledge of the underworld, and he himself was the archetype of the big-business criminal, the organization man controlling the activities of ordinary thieves as well as prostitutes. He was able to exert considerable power over members of the gang with whom he operated, because they depended on him to dispose of their loot; speaking about Peachum to his gang, Macheath says: 'Business cannot go on without him. He is a Man who knows the World, and is a necessary Agent to us. . . . You must continue to act under his Direction, for the moment we break loose from him, our Gang is ruin'd (II.ii). Wild stored ill-gotten gains in his 'Lock', which as Gay explains in a footnote to III.iii was 'A Cant Word, signifying, a Warehouse where stolen Goods are deposited'; Peachum's Lock is the setting for III.v–vi, in which Peachum and Lockit are surrounded by the produce of thieves and pickpockets, especially items stolen during the celebrations to mark the Coronation of George II in October 1727, three months before the first production of the play (they discuss 'The Coronation Account'). Wild frequently returned stolen property to the owners for the rewards they were offering, pretending to be a kind of honest-broker between robbed and robbers and not, of course, revealing that he was the master-mind behind the robbers; the 'Customers' Peachum refers to at the end of I.viii when he instructs Polly to 'Go, talk with 'em' are people in search of stolen goods. Wild also had facilities for sending easily recognizable valuables that could not be safely disposed of in London to the Continent, and Peachum tells Lockit that the jewels obtained at the time of the Coronation are 'so well-known, that they must be sent abroad—You'll find them enter'd under the Article of Exportation'. With so many diverse interests, Wild had to run his business empire very professionally, keeping detailed accounts of all his transactions; account books, which figure prominently in I.i–iii, II.x, and III.v, are Peachum's inseparable companions. In I.iii, for example, Peachum takes stock of his thieves, deciding which ones are bringing in enough to justify their continued existence and which are not. Like any good bourgeois, he is willing to reward industry but determined to punish idleness: 'I hate a lazy Rogue, by whom one can get nothing 'till he is hang'd.' Financial considerations dictate his whole policy, so that he can call an execution 'decent' if he is likely to gain by it. For this reason, Slippery Sam and Tom Tipple are destined to hang, the first because he wants to abandon crime and the second because he is incompetent. Wild himself had no qualms about disposing in this way of criminals who had ceased to be of value to him. Though not a murderer in the usual sense, he probably shared Peachum's view that even murder may be nothing more than a necessary tool for advancing one's commercial interests; 'if Business cannot be carried on without it, what would you have a Gentleman do?', Peachum asks his wife when she is 'whimpring about Murder' in I.iv. But if it was to his advantage, Wild could also save people from the gallows by withholding incriminating evidence. In I.ii, Peachum promises to arrange the acquittal of Betty Sly, who according to Filch 'hath brought more Goods into our Lock to-year than any five of the Gang'; but he remains adamant when Polly, speaking about Macheath, pleads with him to 'sink the material

Evidence, and bring him off at his Tryal' (III.xi). Peachum's only moment
of weakness is when he tells his wife during their discussion about having
Macheath peached that 'it grieves one's Heart to take off a great Man';
but even here he is not thinking simply of Macheath's 'Personal Bravery,
his fine Stratagem', but of all the money 'we have already got by him, and
how much more we may get'. And it is callous of him to hope that his
daughter would do his dirty work for him—'I wish you could have made
Polly undertake it' (I.xi).

Beneath Wild's veneer of respectability and service to the community
in upholding law and order was an unscrupulous and ruthless criminal
devoted largely to self. This is why Wild served Gay's satirical purpose so
well. Wild was the real-life embodiment of the respectable criminal. His
very existence raised doubts about what went on behind other
respectable façades. Peachum's song and short soliloquy that constitute I.i
establish at the outset that a Jonathan Wild is so far from being unique
that he is closer to the norm of human behaviour than most people like to
think. When Peachum compares himself with a lawyer, he finds that
there are no fundamental differences: 'Like me too he acts in a double
Capacity, both against Rogues and for 'em; for 'tis but fitting that we
should protect and encourage Cheats, since we live by them.' It follows
that if law 'is an honest Employment, so is mine'. His complaint in I.iii
that Slippery Sam has 'the Impudence to have views of following his
Trade as a Taylor, which he calls an honest Employment' arises mainly
from Sam's view, naïve in Peachum's eyes, that thieving is more
dishonest than tailoring. But Gay's irony is at its most incisive in Air I,
beginning, 'Through all the Employments of Life / Each Neighbour
abuses his Brother.' In a just world, brothers, whether literal or
metaphorical (as in the case of Peachum and Lockit), would be the last
people to abuse one another, but since in reality they do, the world is
essentially topsy-turvy. There is a profound ambiguity in the third line,
'Whore and Rogue they call Husband and Wife', because it can be read
in two ways: 'Husband and Wife' may be unjustly labelled 'Whore and
Rogue', but equally unjustly 'Whore and Rogue' may be labelled
'Husband and Wife'. The abuse of language is so widespread that words
lose their meanings. The final lines, 'And the Statesman, because he's so
great, / Thinks his Trade as honest as mine', push the absurdity even
further because Peachum is accusing important politicians of suffering
from delusions of honesty and integrity in thinking their activities to be as
honourable as his. Self-deception is part of the terrible price the powerful
pay for their 'greatness', which has nothing whatever to do with

goodness. Even by the standards of the world embodied in Peachum, great statesmen—Walpole was called 'the great man', especially by his political enemies—come off badly. The various references to 'great Man', such as Mrs Peachum's reassuring words to Filch in I.vi that he will be 'a great Man in History' if he avoids public execution, are aimed specifically at Walpole, but do, of course, carry a much wider significance; there are many other satirical allusions to the politician's public and private lives which were obvious enough at the time but need editorial clarification today. For example, the simile in Peachum's declaration that 'My Daughter to me should be, like a Court Lady to a Minister of State, a Key to the whole Gang' (I.iv) alludes to Queen Caroline (wife of George II) and Walpole, who was a particular court favourite of hers. Yet the parallel Gay draws between the wielders of political power and influence and the rulers of a criminal empire does not depend on this specific identification. Though not intended as a straightforward satirical portrait of Walpole, Peachum does correspond to the Whig leader in several ways, and repeatedly draws attention to the favouritism, bribery, and corruption that were certainly not inconspicuous during Walpole's long ministry (1721–42).

Gay concentrates his satire on 'fine Gentlemen' rather than 'fine Ladies', but he does not ignore women or relations between the sexes. By making the ladies of the town act and talk at times like respectable ladies of the beau monde, Gay not only suggests that they have much more in common with one another than is usually thought, but also is able to ridicule aspects of high-society conduct and expose the hypocrisy essential for keeping up appearances. The significance of the closing lines of II.vi may not be immediately obvious if the play is read and not seen; in fact, two prostitutes, Mrs Slammekin and Dolly Trull, are trying to out-do each other in courtesy over who should go first through the door of a disreputable tavern. Considering what and where they are, their language is absurdly inflated, Mrs Slammekin's ''Tis impossible for me' and 'Nay, then I must stay here all Night' matching Dolly Trull's 'I would not for the World' and 'As I hope to be sav'd, Madam' in silly, hyperbolic extravagance; even sillier is that having just had a disagreement they are desperately trying to score off each other. Yet the mock-heroic incongruity only goes to show that such behaviour over so trivial a matter would be ludicrous in any social context, including high society, which often takes such inane niceties seriously, and furthermore that politesse is for the most part a sham and can even be a mask for rancour.

When the prostitutes arrive at the tavern in II.iv, Macheath addresses them with words that immediately connect polite society with them: 'all you fine Ladies, who know your own Beauty, affect an Undress.' The whores' style of clothing is obviously designed to advertise their sexual wares, but in hinting that 'fine Ladies' also dress to display their physical attributes to best advantage in order to tantalize men, he is suggesting that the behaviour of upper-class women is no less sexually motivated. But whereas most of the whores make no attempt to disguise what they are up to, 'fine Ladies' would no doubt run a mile from anyone so ungentlemanly as to point to this truth in public. It would be a different matter in private, hypocrisy being inescapable in polite circles. Greeting Jenny Diver who is 'As prim and demure as ever', Macheath calls her 'a dear artful Hypocrite' because 'There is not any Prude, though ever so high bred, hath a more sanctify'd Look, with a more mischievous Heart'. Yet if a prostitute can assume the appearance of an upper-class prude in public, there is no reason why a prude should not be as promiscuous as a prostitute—in private of course. When Macheath orders drinks for the prostitutes, he urges them not to be coy about ordering spirits if that is what they want, only to be told by Jenny Diver that 'I never drink Strong-Waters, but when I have the Cholic'. Macheath recognizes that she is playing the prude, because this is 'Just the Excuse of the fine Ladies' to justify their gin-drinking, which was otherwise regarded as low and vulgar in the extreme. According to Macheath, 'a Lady of Quality is never without the Cholic' and so never without spirits—for medical reasons. In making Jenny protect her public image by behaving so decorously, Gay is ridiculing not her but the 'fine Ladies' who hide their weaknesses and dissipations behind a mask of virtue.

Gay continues his attack on the hypocrisy of 'fine Ladies' in III.viii, when Lucy tries to persuade Polly to take a strong alcoholic drink, which is in fact poisoned. 'Not the greatest Lady in the Land could have better in her Closet, for her own private drinking', declares Lucy, who reveals how such a lady would act in public when she accuses the reluctant Polly of being as 'squeamishly affected about taking a Cup of Strong-Waters as a Lady before Company' (III.x). To enjoy drink and sex, two of women's greatest delights, is one thing; to admit to enjoying them, or even to indulging in them, is quite another. Even Polly adds to the satire of high-society women. As an example of how Polly 'loves to imitate the fine Ladies', her mother explains to her father that she allows Macheath to take liberties with her 'in the View of Interest', for purely selfish or business reasons (I.iv). Although this indicates a total failure on

Mrs Peachum's part to understand her daughter's motives, it allows Gay to accuse 'fine Ladies' of seldom acting except out of self-interest. The assumption behind Polly's own remark to her father, 'A Woman knows how to be mercenary, though she hath never been in a Court or at an Assembly' (an assembly was a fashionable social gathering), is that while being mercenary is not the preserve of the upper classes, it is so closely identified with them that it can be taken for granted as a *sine qua non* (I.vii). As for Mrs Peachum, she acts out the part of a gentlewoman and respectable businessman's wife so completely that she illustrates the hypocrisy of 'fine Ladies' as well as anyone. Shortly after telling her husband, 'I never meddle in matters of Death; I always leave those Affairs to you' (I.iv), she seems upset by his talk of murder, claiming that she cannot 'help the Frailty of an over-scrupulous Conscience'. Yet later in Act I when she learns of Polly's marriage, she does 'meddle in matters of Death' by pressing her husband to arrange Macheath's trial and execution as soon as possible, her 'over-scrupulous Conscience' forgotten. For a fine lady, an 'over-scrupulous Conscience' would appear to be an affectation which it is pleasant to indulge when there is nothing at stake but which evaporates when envy, anger, or self-interest are aroused.

Finally, Gay's satire on love and marriage in high society is mainly concentrated in the scenes in which Polly is confronted by her parents after their discovery of her marriage. These scenes have already been discussed in detail in connection with romance and anti-romance, and little need be said here, but the fact that the same episodes can be discussed under different headings—and these scenes also play a part in the burlesque of Italian opera—indicates how superbly integrated the different elements of the play are. The Peachums' social affectation and pretence to gentility are nowhere more plain than when Mrs Peachum appeals to Filch to reveal the truth about Polly because 'the Honour of our Family is concern'd' (I.vi), or when Peachum advises his wife not to let her anger at the disclosures 'break through the Rules of Decency' (I.viii), or when Mrs Peachum complains that 'all the Hopes of our Family are gone for ever and ever' because her daughter has married a criminal (I.viii). The height of Mrs Peachum's bourgeois primness is probably her self-pitying eruption: 'How the Mother is to be pitied who hath handsome Daughters! Locks, Bolts, Bars, and Lectures of Morality are nothing to them: They break through them all' (I.viii). She could have tolerated an affair between Polly and Macheath because 'the very best Families have excus'd and huddled up a Frailty of that sort'; pre-marital sex like extra-marital sex ('And why must Polly's Marriage, contrary to all Observation, make her the less followed by other Men?' (I.v)) is clearly not a serious fault unless it is found out. And she would not have objected to Polly's marrying 'a Person of Distinction' for money or social position (I.viii). But to marry anyone for love, let alone a criminal, is the last straw. 'I thought the Girl had been better bred', says the distraught Mrs Peachum as she collapses in I.viii, implying that no really well-bred girl from the aristocracy or gentry would consider marrying except for money or position. Marriage among the upper classes would seem to be a business deal totally unconnected with love, which can be sought, even if it cannot be found, outside marriage. If Polly believes she is behaving 'like the Gentry' in marrying Macheath, she is deluding herself about what that entails and will have to accept the consequences outlined by her mother:

> Can you support the Expence of a Husband, Hussy, in gaming, drinking and whoring? have you Money enough to carry on the daily Quarrels of Man and Wife about who shall squander most? There are not many Husbands and Wives, who can bear the Charges of plaguing one another in a handsome way. (I.viii)

Marriage is a form of duelling, the most satisfactory outcome for the woman being the early demise of her husband—'The comfortable Estate of Widow-hood, is the only Hope that keeps up a Wife's Spirits' (I.x). Through the Peachums, Gay lays bare the far from charming realities behind the glittering exteriors of some high-society marriages. Even Polly's parents do not regard her marriage to a highwayman as likely to be any worse than her marriage to a peer would have been, and there is the positive advantage that criminals are more easily disposed of than lords.

5 Conclusion

For all its comic and witty dialogue, The Beggar's Opera is much more than the light-hearted romp with a certain period charm that some modern producers have turned it into. There is a flippant side to the play, but Gay's contemporaries would not have made the mistake of failing to see the fundamental seriousness for the surface humour. For them, the numerous allusions to well-known people of the time, whether singers like Francesca Cuzzoni, politicians like Walpole, or criminals like Wild, as well as to current events such as George II's Coronation (III.v) and to recently enacted legislation like 'The Act for destroying the Mint' and 'the Act too against Imprisonment for small Sums', which Mrs Trapes complains about in III.vi, would have fixed the play very firmly in the contemporary world of the 1720s. *The Beggar's Opera* is far too comically stylized to be 'realistic', but it is very much about the real world. The characters are windows opening onto a panorama of society, so that in addition to seeing them as solid dramatic figures in their own right, we see through them into a wide range of human experience. For this reason, we regard even the villains of the piece, Peachum and Lockit, with some indulgence, not only because they are comic creations but because their stage villainy is a pale reflection of real-life villainy. Gay's widespread use of topical references helped to make his satire immediately accessible to his contemporaries, but he is not writing ephemeral local satire any more than Pope is in *The Rape of the Lock* and *The Dunciad* or Swift is in *Gulliver's Travels*. Gay, like Pope and Swift, uses contemporary examples to illustrate universal themes. Pope did settle some personal scores by putting his enemies in *The Dunciad*, but he is not so much concerned with Grub Street hacks as with what they represent. The Goddess of Dulness whom they serve is a permanent threat to civilization, not just to Augustan values and society. Gay, too, is dealing with human nature and society in general rather than with the England of George I, Walpole, Handel, and Wild. Indeed, one of the effects of the comic stylization is to lift the play out of its immediate 1720s context and so universalize it.

There are other advantages in Gay's comic and ironic approach to the diseases of civilization. It allowed him to mount a full-scale offensive on the public, political, and court life of the time while pretending that he was doing no such thing. This resembles the indirect attacks employing allegory or fable that have been made against totalitarian régimes by modern writers living under them. More significantly, Gay, like the best of his contemporaries, knew that the rapier usually proved to be a more effective weapon than the bludgeon. Gay could have written a grimly realistic play about the greed, predatoriness, and self-interest motivating much human behaviour from the court to the parish of St Giles-in-the-Fields, and about the hypocrisy and sham veneers used, especially by the upper classes, to disguise their essential baseness. But such an approach would have been portentous, self-righteous, and fairly easy to resist. Gay was fully aware that a well-aimed witticism could be much more devastating than a sermon. His comic method of attack has a lulling and ingratiating effect even on those most under fire so that they are caught with their defences down. As a spokesman for the Augustan values of reason, moderation, and good sense, Gay believed in the moral function of satire as an instrument for exposing folly and vice and so for correcting all those deviations from the standards he upheld.

Yet there is something radically unsettling about *The Beggar's Opera*. Almost as soon as it reached the stage, moralists attacked it for glamourizing crime and prostitution and for violating all the accepted values of respectable society, and such attacks continued into the nineteenth century. This view of the play is very shallow, because Gay is certainly not glamourizing or even defending crime and prostitution but using them to question respectable society itself and its accepted values. Gay turns the world upside down, not to demonstrate, as a Romantic author might have done, that criminals are morally superior to aristocrats and politicians but that aristrocrats and politicians are often no better than criminals. Macheath is no paragon and does not represent an ideal—he belongs more to the mock-heroic than to the heroic world—but he is certainly no worse than many of those taken for granted in society as his 'betters'. The whole basis of law and social morality may seem secure and unshakeable to the dominant classes, but Gay undermines that belief in order to shatter the dogmatism, smugness, and complacency of those classes and to bring to light the discrepancy between appearance and reality in high society. Gay is not an anarchist or revolutionary attempting to destroy the existing order of society, but a reformer trying to put the existing order of society back on the right lines.

One of the most modern features of the play is that it leaves us uncertain about the reliability of language itself, just as do many modern writers like Samuel Beckett and other dramatists of the Absurd. If highwaymen can speak like courtiers, and ringleaders of crime like politicians or respectable businessmen, is there any truth in words? Should we believe what anyone says? When crime is 'Business', when robbers are 'Sound Men, and true', when a thief 'saves' goods from fires, when a criminal is a 'Villain' because he wants to abandon crime, when prostitutes are 'fine Ladies', and when making female felons pregnant to save them from the death sentence is an 'honest Livelyhood', the firm floor of language seems to give way beneath our feet like a trapdoor. In I.ii, Filch speaks of 'Penitence' as a weakness that is likely to break a man's spirit, and in I.vi Mrs Peachum tells Filch that she thought he had 'lost

Fear as well as Shame' as though both were childhood phobias that one grows out of. Words like 'great' and 'honest' are misused so systematically by the characters that language does become untrustworthy. Words go out of focus, as it were, so that we are no longer sure of what they mean. Indeed, the abuse of language becomes so normal that it is perhaps an abuse of language to talk about 'the abuse of language'. All this is amusing, but the humour is also very disturbing. Far from providing us with any certainties, Gay leaves us disorientated, stripped of our prejudices and conventional attitudes so that we have to find our bearings by looking more deeply into ourselves, our social environment, and our language. Yet he manages to achieve this by captivating us with a witty, exuberant, and brilliantly theatrical musical play. Gay's freewheeling, almost Brechtian, blend of comedy and pathos, burlesque and realism, speech and song, which defies neo-classical orthodoxy and prefigures the deliberate blurring of genres and styles in the more adventurous drama of the twentieth century, does at least fulfil the neo-classical stipulation that art should delight as well as instruct.

Bibliography

CRITICAL EDITIONS

ed. G. C. Faber, in *The Poetical Works of John Gay* (London 1926).

ed. G. H. Nettleton and A. E. Case, in *British Dramatists from Dryden to Sheridan* (Boston 1939), revised by G. W. Stone (1969).

ed. E. V. Roberts (Lincoln, Nebraska 1968; London 1969) for the Regents Restoration Drama Series with an introductory essay, notes and music.

ed. P. E. Lewis (Edinburgh 1973) with introduction, commentary and bibliography.

Also important is the facsimile of the third edition of 1729 with commentaries by L. Kronenberger and M. Goberman (Larchmont, New York 1961).

CRITICISM

S. M. Armens, *John Gay, Social Critic* (New York 1954).

A. V. Berger, 'The Beggar's Opera, the Burlesque, and Italian Opera', *Music and Letters* XVII (1936).

B. H. Bronson, 'The Beggar's Opera' in *Studies in the Comic* (Berkeley and Los Angeles 1941); reprinted in *Restoration Drama: Modern Essays in Criticism*, ed. J. Loftis (New York 1966).

C. F. Burgess, 'The Genesis of The Beggar's Opera', *Cithara* II (1962).

——'Political Satire: John Gay's The Beggar's Opera', *Midwest Quarterly* VI (1965).

I. Donaldson, '"A Double Capacity": The Beggar's Opera' in *The World Upside-Down: Comedy from Jonson to Fielding* (Oxford 1970).

W. Empson, 'The Beggar's Opera' in *Some Versions of Pastoral* (London 1935).

E. M. Gagey, *Ballad Opera* (New York 1937).

G. Handley-Taylor and F. G. Barker, *John Gay and the Ballad Opera* (London 1956).

J. Preston, 'The Ironic Mode: A Comparison of *Jonathan Wild* and *The Beggar's Opera*', *Essays in Criticism* XVI (1966).

J. O. Rees, '"A Great Man in Distress": Macheath as Hercules', *University of Colorado Studies, Series in Language and Literature* X (1966).

W. E. Schultz, *Gay's 'Beggar's Opera': Its Content, History and Influence* (New Haven 1923).

P. M. Spacks, *John Gay* (New York 1965).

The best biography of Gay is *John Gay, Favorite of the Wits* (Durham, North Carolina 1940) by W. H. Irving, whose *John Gay's London* (Cambridge, Massachussetts 1928) remains one of the best studies of Gay's milieu. The most recent edition of Gay's *Letters* is by C. F. Burgess (Oxford 1966).

Index

Already published in the series: